Be the Bombshell

REBECCA JENNINGS

SIMON & SCHUSTER

New York   Amsterdam/Antwerp   London
Toronto   Sydney/Melbourne   New Delhi

An Imprint of Simon & Schuster, LLC
1230 Avenue of the Americas
New York, NY 10020

First Simon & Schuster trade paperback edition May 2025

SIMON & SCHUSTER PAPERBACKS and colophon are registered trademarks of Simon & Schuster, LLC

Interior design by Wendy Blum

Manufactured in the United States of America

10 9 8 7 6 5 4 3 2 1

Library of Congress Cataloging-in-Publication Data has been applied for.

ISBN 978-1-6682-0564-8
ISBN 978-1-6682-0565-5 (ebook)

Contents

FOR THE GROUP CHATS <3

Be the Bombshell

Introduction

(OR WELCOME TO THE VILLA)

It was while watching *Love Island* series 5—still the most watched to this day, and by many accounts the best season of all time—that I realized something was very, very wrong. The hottest woman I've ever seen in my life had just entered the villa, and for some mysterious reason, horrible things kept happening to her.

The first boy she fancied chose to stay with his existing partner over recoupling with her, even after saying he'd want her "gift wrapped." Then she overheard another boy—one she ended up settling for—making a gross joke at her expense. In Casa Amor, she entertained a brief fling that fizzled almost immediately. Finally, she ended the series with a guy who'd just made an ass of himself for breaking up with a girl who was deeply in love with him. It was the same guy she'd later allege cheated on her months after the show ended. (The guy, for his part, has denied doing so.)

Her name, of course, is Maura Higgins, one of the most iconic cast members to have ever graced the *Love Island* villa. And it was while watching her repeatedly try and fail to find a decent dude over the course of eight weeks that I realized modern dating is totally, utterly fucked. If someone like Maura, whom both her fellow islanders and audiences adored—and who happens to look like *that*—didn't end the series with the love of her life, then what hope do the rest of us have?

I'm not saying that the exceptionally gorgeous among us are owed the most amount of happiness. But *Love Island* favors the beautiful, the sexy, the hottest of the hot. And when the system designed to work for a very specific type of person *doesn't even work for them*, it means perhaps that system isn't very useful to begin with.

If you're currently single, there's a system, too—and you know what I'm referring to here. I'm talking about the *apps*, specifically the apps that turn human beings into avatars on a screen you have to swipe through like it's your job in order to find someone you might theoretically be interested in grabbing a drink with.

Love Island is a microcosm of this system. It mimics the persistent feeling on dating apps of convincing yourself that someone "better" might come along by creating a revolving door of new islanders and voting out ones who aren't paired up. Don't like your current partner? Just wait a few days for a "hot new bombshell" to enter the villa! The same goes for the apps: Your date gives you the ick? Kick 'em to the curb and keep swiping, baby! In the same way *Love Island* functions primarily as entertainment rather than a genuine attempt at matchmaking, dating apps have become casinos, demanding ever more of your time and money to fulfill the promises they market themselves with.

But there's a crucial exception to the parallel between these two worlds. While dating apps function in the infinite ether of the internet, the titular island is a physical place, bound by the constraints of human interaction and the dimensions of your average pool. On *Love Island*, you can't switch seamlessly between twelve different dudes' texts asking "wyd" and have the most boring conversation of your life for the rest of time. You have to actually talk to them face-to-face and find a way to politely maneuver the conversation, see if you're compatible, and date, rather than doing the good ol' unmatch-and-ghost.

When you realize this, you understand why so many people like Maura—people who seem like they could walk into any room and have even the walls fall in love with them—keep going on *Love Island*, beyond the prospect of a zillion Instagram followers. To be on *Love Island* is to live in a fantasy world with no algorithms and no apps that demand you pay yet another fee to see the people you really like. It is to live and breathe and eat and play inside an exclusive singles bar for two months straight. And it is to sidestep all the worst parts of app-based dating: the radio silence (you can't escape someone who's sleeping in the bed next to you!), the regrettable drunken hookups (contestants are limited to two drinks a day), and the constant bids from apps to get you to spend even more money by dangling the prospect of The One (instead, you're the one getting paid!). It's entertainment, sure, but it's also a social experiment that reimagines a different way to date at a time when dating feels uniquely inhuman.

It's no wonder why personalized matchmaking services and IRL singles events and flirty run clubs are having such a moment right now. People are longing to meet the old-fashioned way, but so many don't know how or where to start. They feel like they can't or don't want to approach people in public because face-to-face rejection is too horrifying to imagine. They feel like the only people who are into them are the ones they're a little repulsed by. They feel like the people they *are* into only see them as pixels on a screen, a virtual pen pal to lead on for a few days or weeks and then ignore when they find someone better.

This is not entirely the fault of Big Dating App. People are becoming lonelier and more isolated in general thanks to the decline of social clubs and religious and civic organizations over the past sixty-odd years. Instead we spend more time working, commuting, and consuming media by ourselves, making us more focused on our individual needs and less likely to trust strangers. "Trustworthiness lubricates social life," wrote Robert Putnam in *Bowling Alone*, his 2000 book on the collapse of American community. Without it, we're all just awkwardly sitting around and glaring at each other, refusing to speak to anyone and getting frustrated that nobody's willing to come up and talk to us.

And it's not like we've had particularly excellent role models in pop culture. Those of us who grew up on Disney movies and rom-coms where the quirky, overworked, lovable klutz ends up with the roguishly handsome and conveniently rich guy know these films aren't documentaries or based remotely in any factual truth, but they do an incredible job at selling us on the idea that they could be. They teach us that enemies really *could* become lovers, that when a man is sort of mean to you, that just means he *likes* you, that any man who (a) lives in a small town, (b) is hot but doesn't know it, or (c) has some sort of quaint or old-timey job such as carpentry or writing about sports for his local newspaper is actually the love of your life and will never hurt you. (From this, we can also infer that hot finance guys from New York are evil and will ruin your life, which is true, actually.)

And then there are those other popular reality TV shows about finding love, *The Bachelor* and *Love Is Blind*, both of which are almost comically earnest and self-serious about the idea that what you are watching is *true love* and not a bunch of contestants being placed into a Stanford Prison Experiment–like solitary confinement and who may or may not be the victims of severe labor violations. Both shows are designed for a precise narrative arc: A couple meets, falls in love, and then, in order to prove to the world how real their love is, must get married, or at the very least engaged, before the cameras stop rolling. This is for the same reason pretty much all rom-coms end in weddings: It's the only way audiences can walk away without a doubt that their protagonists ended up happily ever after.

All of modern pop culture's portrayals of love and partnership, from Netflix Christmas movies to romantasy novels to Disney to *The Bachelor*, sell us on the fantasy that monogamous romantic love is the only means of achieving a fulfilling life. It also sells us on the notion that once you find it, the rest of your life will fall seamlessly into place, that it will set you on a track that signals to the rest of the world that you're doing great and will continue to do great forever (just as long as you get married and have kids and follow in the footsteps of every conventional norm we're supposed to aspire to).

So we're left with dating apps that promise to solve all these problems and connect you with real people who might genuinely like you back. Yet we still end up lonely and confused, dulling our senses to the romantic escapades we could be participating in out in the real world.

This isn't an anti-app book—I met my husband on Hinge, and therefore will forever be in its debt. (Match Group, if you would like to spend some of your billions of dollars on sponsoring me, I promise I will say nothing bad about you for the rest of this book.) But that was back in 2018, practically the ancient times for online dating, before the pandemic made everything weird and fraught and before anyone had ever heard the concept of "rose jail" (if you don't know what this is, consider yourself among the very fortunate).

Instead, this is a book that will help you get out of the rut that apps and other conventions of contemporary dating force us into. It's a book that will make dating actually fun again—to open your eyes to the potential of meeting spontaneously, talking to strangers, falling in love, raising your standards, dropping people (respectfully!) who don't deserve you, and finding yourself in the process.

I can't promise you'll find the love of your life at the end of this book. No one can promise that. But you *will* be able to learn from the lessons of the many islanders who came before you, women like *Love Island* US's Kaylor, who wore her heart on her sleeve and spent her entire season trying to make it work with someone at the expense of her own dignity. As difficult as it was to watch, so many of us saw ourselves in her, having been the Kaylor in relationships past. Which made it all the more satisfying to see her emerge from the villa as a more confident and self-possessed person with a new best friend by her side.

That's the goal here. To leave you glowing and more sure of yourself than you've ever felt before—whether you're in a couple or not.

For the past decade, I've been a journalist covering pop culture—and, of course, a huge fan of *Love Island*. I'm fascinated by the ways in which reality television accurately (or sometimes inaccurately) reflects our lives. And as for dating, I don't think there's a single better show than *Love Island* that mirrors what it's actually like to be in these streets as a single person who's casually dating, excited about the prospect of meeting "their person" but not expecting it to happen right this minute.

One of the most refreshing things about *Love Island* is that it doesn't try to sell you on the fiction of a heteronormative, happily-ever-after white wedding. Viewers are well aware that what we're watching is hot people in the least amount of clothing possible flirting with each other. When I interviewed *Love Island* US's executive producer Simon Thomas for an article, "How *Love Island USA* Became This Summer's Most Exquisite Trash," in 2024, he told me that the show takes a fundamental "sex-positive, pro-sex approach" that many American television shows are either too fearful or too prudish to adopt. "We're not coupling you up to get married, like some sort of puritanical goal of like, if you're having fun in the sun, you must get married at the end of it. That's not the purpose of this," he said.

That *Love Island* might seem on the surface frothy and frivolous conceals the fact that it is in many ways packed with much less artifice than its counterparts. Sure, the elements of the show that tend to get the most attention are the ones that take this superficiality to its extreme—like, for instance, that time one contestant thought the county of Essex was a continent, or when an islander said his greatest desire in life was to do sponcon for Cheez-Its. But at the same time, the show is compelling because of how true to life it is, underneath the fake tan and veneers. Below the surface, the people who enter and leave the villa are no different than the people you're swiping on the apps or the friends-of-friends you meet at parties. In other words, the majority of them are normal people in their own dating trenches. They're frustrated by the same bad behavior and flaky mentality that have made you lose hope. They're looking for someone kind, someone hilarious, someone respectful and fun to be around, and they're wondering why that feels so damn impossible to find. *Love Island* is a piece of pop culture that should be taken seriously, with plenty to say about modern love, dating, and friendship. For that reason, it's a perfect jumping-off point to talk about the state of dating right now, and how we can make it even better.

My hope is that you, presumable *Love Island* fan, can find something just as valuable in this book. I hope it inspires you to break out of habits you've found yourself stuck in, to demand what you want without apology, to meet people where they're at and learn to tell the difference between knowing what's worth the compromise and what's settling for less than you deserve. I hope it challenges you to think outside your "type on paper" and not be afraid to crack on with a stranger IRL. I hope it offers guidance when you feel like a "mug" or that you're constantly being voted off the proverbial island. I hope it encourages you to feel like the absolute ten-out-of-ten, proper fit, total bombshell that you are.

Mostly I want you to feel as though in the process of all that, you have your very own group chat to help navigate the best, worst, and weirdest part of dating. And to do so, I've tapped my very own group chats for their hard-won wisdom. I'm incredibly lucky to have so many delightful, strong, and cool people in my life willing to share their stories and advice, and I hope that as you read through this book, the stories of these everyday people form a little Greek chorus—or perhaps your own villa—in your head just as they do in mine, reminding you that dating is hard but shouldn't be an intolerable part of life. Dating can and should be fun, fulfilling, and empowering.

A little disclaimer: The vast majority of the examples we're going to be talking about in this book are heterosexual. That doesn't mean there aren't useful lessons to learn for everyone, but overall *Love Island* is mostly a show about straight people. (But not always! See chapter 13!)

I know it feels rough out there right now. You can be Maura Higgins and it's *still* rough out there. But what if there was a place we could all go, a place where the rules of contemporary dating are subverted in a way that makes everything shinier, sunnier, more fun? A place that forces you to get offline and actually flex your flirting muscles for once? A place where you have just as much likelihood of finding friendship and fulfillment as the love of your life?

That place exists. For some, it's Mallorca. For others, it's Fiji. Maybe for you it's the local dive bar trivia night, or maybe it's the café with the cute barista. Wherever it is, it's *your* island, and you're both the director and the star.

So get ready. A hot new bombshell has just arrived.

One

ARE THEY YOUR "TYPE ON PAPER," OR ARE THEY A SAD PHOTOCOPY?

In the premiere episode of *Love Island* season 8, the islanders and audience alike were surprised by something never before heard on the show: a smoldering Italian accent, courtesy of one Davide Sanclimenti. Sanclimenti, whose physical appearance defies description but is basically what would happen if a Roman statue went on steroids, was a departure from the typical *Love Island* contestant in more ways than one. When asked what his "type" is, he replies in his charmingly broken English, "The color of the hair, I mean, I don't fall in love because how old are you or if you are blonde or a brunette, I fall in love for the personality."

Few statements could be so shocking in such an environment. On *Love Island*, contestants constantly talk about their "type on paper," a refrain you'll hear a whole lot on the show. (Do NOT play a drinking game where you have to take a shot every time you hear the phrase. You will die.) Almost all the men will describe their perfect woman in the form of hair color, meaning either "blonde" or "brunette" (because these are the only shades of hair men recognize), and almost all the women will say their type is "tall, dark, and handsome." And yes, there will always be exactly one blonde man standing alone, destined to couple up with the only solo girl left.

At the beginning of each season (or "series" as they call it in the far superior UK version), that "type on paper" is all the contestants have to go on, and this forms the basis of every premiere: A group of impossibly hunky and gorgeous singles gather on a tropical island, wearing the least amount of clothing humanly possible, and decide who among their fellow contestants of the opposite sex they'd like to "couple up" with. "Coupling up" is the primary mechanism of how the show functions: If you're in a couple, you share a bed, compete in challenges, and ultimately vie for a £50,000 prize (or an even heftier $100,000 in the American show) by performing your compatibility to the voting public.

A typical *Love Island* premiere unfolds with six mostly barechested men in shorts entering the villa, one by one, while the six women already there get to decide which of the men they're into. It's pure pageantry, you can almost *feel* the fact that every dude was furiously doing push-ups off camera. Usually, the women, standing in a row, will take one step forward to indicate their interest in the man walking in—which they can do even if they're already coupled up with someone and a hotter guy arrives. Humiliating? Sure. Entertaining? Absolutely.

As heavily produced as it is, that doesn't mean what happens on day one of the *Love Island* villa is wholly unrealistic. It is, in fact, a microcosm of online dating, where at any moment, you could be replaced by someone else on the app: The pool is much bigger, but most of the time, what makes a person want to couple up with someone else is a first impression. An example: Perhaps someone includes a picture of themselves on their dating profile wearing a newsboy cap, and you're forced to wonder whether it's part of a Halloween costume or if they earnestly think this is, like, a good look for them. Or they're still using those heavily saturated photo filters circa Instagram 2016. Like the islanders, all we have to go on are our most superficial judgments about the men and women shown to us, shaped by deep-rooted ideas about our "type on paper," or villa vernacular for a person's physical preference.

It's lucky for the islanders that the absolute bare minimum requirement to be on *Love Island* is to be hot. And it's lucky for us, the audience, because as judgmental as we might consider the islanders who flock to only the tallest, most muscular men or the women with the plumpest lips (seriously, what are they doing over there in the UK? Is Juvéderm covered by the NHS?!), we're judging them just as much as they're judging each other.

We all have a type on paper. A friend once described mine as "tall and fluffy," an entirely correct assessment of the fact that for as long as she'd known me, I'd only ever dated men above six feet who possessed what might be called "dad bods," which I would consider extremely hot. (We as a society must fight against the notion that visible abs are hotter than muscular arms and legs.) She could have read me even more scathingly if she'd wanted to, though: Not only did I exclusively date big guys, I only dated big guys who wrote professionally—or at least aspired to—who wore glasses, and who had intellectually nerdy mannerisms that translated into an encyclopedic knowledge of sports, even when they weren't jocks themselves. They were usually on the anxious side of the anxious-depressed spectrum, had good heads of hair, and made me laugh. (Swap out the glasses and trade the sports for reality television and I'm basically describing myself, but we don't need to psychoanalyze the reasons for that right now.)

All of which is to say that I truly do understand these professionally hot aspiring influencers who populate the *Love Island* villa, the ones with strict rules about how many tattoos are too many and what counts as "natural-looking" veneers. But I'm here to tell you that your type on paper is a lie.

It's not real! You're telling me that you are *only* interested in men over six feet with brown eyes and the "right" amount of tattoos on his arms? You wouldn't date someone who's five foot eleven?

Choosing dates based on "your type" excludes a whole set of people whom you might be compatible with in all the actually important ways that could lead to a meaningful relationship.

As Tara Suwinyattichaiporn, a professor of sexual communication at California State University, Fullerton, explains, your "type" is a "combination of things that [you] have come across throughout your life that you've somehow become drawn to," be it from your environment and culture, your peers, and, yes, the media. "People's types are often based on the cultural beauty standards of where you are from," she says.

It also, of course, comes from your own past experiences—maybe your parents had a great marriage, and your dad was super outdoorsy, and therefore you've unconsciously associated "good relationship" with "lots of camping," when in reality camping is stupid and bad. "When [you] meet someone who seems to fit every single characteristic that you are looking for, you want to make it work so badly that [you might] overvalue this person," adds Betsy Chung, clinical psychologist and author of *The Couple Skills Workbook*.

The solution? Break out of this restrictive approach to dating by being open to different types of people. The next time you're swiping, don't just look at the photos—read the prompts and use them to your advantage, either to fuel your arsenal of smooth conversation starters or to find another source of compatibility that feels authentic to you beyond a potentially shorter man than you're used to dating. A little risk can be the exact thing you need to give your dating life the freshness it's desperate for.

Not only does sticking to your type tie you to repeating patterns of the past, but you're also closing yourself off to people who might make a much better fit for you in the long term. My friend Zoe, for instance, had a strict rule about never dating anyone younger than she was. Then she started hanging out with a coworker named Jake who was seven months younger than her—but only as friends because, well, he was younger.

Still, Zoe had a ton of fun with him. One night they found themselves at a bar grabbing food, and Jake mentioned a twenty-four-hour casino an hour and a half away they should go to sometime. "I was like, 'Why don't we just go tonight?'" she recalls. Despite the fact that it was close to midnight and they both had to work an early shift the next morning, they drove all the way there, arriving at one a.m. and staying out until six, singing to the radio and grabbing McDonald's on the way back. "You know when you click with somebody, and you just want to spend all your time with them, and you can do anything with them and it's a good time? It was just so fun." Jake was *right* for Zoe. He was kind, funny, and adventurous—all important values for her.

Eventually, of course, Zoe realized that the seven-month "issue" wasn't an issue at all, and thirteen years later, they're now happily married. But they never would have matched on a dating app. Zoe, like a lot of women do, would have set her algorithm to only include people her own age or older. But like, imagine missing out on your husband because of a *seven*-month age gap?!

Note that Zoe chose Jake based on the qualities of his personality, not by her "on paper" standards. Part of the problem with a type is that it prevents us from looking long enough at the other person to see if they have the actually important qualities like kindness, consistency, and stability and has us instead making snap judgments based on their appearance (which, let's be real, appearances can and will change!).

The producers on *Love Island* know this, and play with the islanders' and audience's expectations. Anytime it seems like two contestants are cracking on a little bit too well, they'll introduce a bombshell who's *exactly* one of their types on paper in an effort to shake things up. Yet often, the couples we root for the most are the ones who are happy and loved-up despite not really being their usual types. That's because it's a sign the islanders went beyond the superficial and really got to know one another and ended up happier for it. The same should be said for your own approach the next time you're swiping.

And then there are the patterns we find ourselves stuck in, where we feel like we're dating the same type over and over again even though we know it's bad for us. Consider the old standby: the girl who only dates "bad boys." (I hate this term, it's infantilizing! These are grown men who are fully capable of behaving normally and yet refuse to do so! Therefore, I humbly propose we rebrand the "bad boy" as the Shitty Grown Man.) She can't help it. Normal, kind, sane men just don't do it for her. Instead, she's into the guy who gives her just enough attention to maintain her interest, but not enough to ever actually define the relationship. He'll lay it on thick when he wants something, then act like she's crazy for taking this as legitimate enthusiasm. Worse, whenever an emotionally healthy dude shows actual interest in her, she's weirded out and turned off.

There's a reason why so many women find themselves attracted to men like, say, Adam Collard, who was a menace on both *Love Island* seasons 4 and 8. Yes, he was extremely hot. And it's not a crime to couple up with a bunch of different women in quick succession on a show like *Love Island*. But he was also accused of gaslighting his partner Rosie when she complained he was ignoring her in favor of the new girl, Zara, to the point that women's charities were releasing statements on his problematic behavior. The difference between being a guy who dates multiple people casually and a Shitty Grown Man is that a Shitty Grown Man won't be forthright when he's seeing someone else (or is interested in doing so). I know it's hard, but try not to get caught in the toxic, albeit sometimes admittedly pleasurable, cycle of dating the Shitty Grown Man. It's never worth it in the end.

We fall into these patterns for many reasons, but part of dating is learning to both heal and grow beyond the inner wounds that lie to us about what we really want out of dating and love. Don't fault yourself for not having the best example of a positive, loving, and healthy relationship in your childhood—work through the old, stubborn beliefs as the first step to ending the same tired cycle. Let go of the Shitty Grown Man: He doesn't fulfill the actual underlying needs to build a healthy, lasting relationship.

Lest you assume I'm being harsh, here is where I will divulge an embarrassing secret: Once, in a dark moment after breaking up with someone who fit my type on paper almost too well, I altered my Hinge settings so that I could *only* be matched up with a person who looked, in all respects, exactly like him. This was a very weird experiment that led me to scroll through a bunch of uncanny valley versions of my ex, only to be reaffirmed how much they were *not* him after I went on dates with a few of them. Instead, they were sad photocopies of my type on paper, men who left me feeling even lonelier than before.

It wasn't fair to those guys—they were people! Real, actual people, not amalgams of my own delusional projections, or items to check off on a grocery list. Dating apps have effectively incentivized the endless typification of other people. Not only do they give us tools to weed out potential dates by height, body type, race, or any other superficial category you can think of, but they also use algorithms to pair people up who match each other's preferences. This isn't necessarily a bad thing, of course, but rather a shallow one: efficiency at the expense of serendipity. Who might I date, I wondered, if I couldn't simply filter out everyone who wasn't "my type"?

Much like algorithms that use collaborative filtering to suss out what individual users might most like to watch on a streaming service, we as daters tend to use our type on paper to narrow down our options in an unfathomably huge pool of fellow singles. It's the most understandable thing in the world, but it's also possible that it's doing us a disservice.

Even the newer tools added by dating app companies to improve user experience haven't always helped. The ability to list certain qualities as "dealbreakers," for instance, is theoretically useful for saving time on a go-nowhere first date, but it ignores the fact that, in many cases, people aren't really that great at figuring out what they want. As much as the apps try to help make it clear what people are looking for by including a dedicated section for listing it, the available answers—"open to short- and long-term relationships" and "figuring out dating goals"—are, at best, vague, and not always aligned with how people actually date.

But just because we're not great at knowing what we want doesn't mean we're powerless to get it. Whenever a friend is debating whether to go on a second or third date with someone they're unsure about, I almost always encourage them to give it another shot. Attraction takes time, and there won't always be fireworks on a first date. First dates are famously terrible! They are an investment of your time, money, and energy, and when it doesn't turn out perfectly, it feels like you've wasted all three. You're basically settling in for a business meeting, but instead of business you're deciding whether you want to put your mouth on that person's mouth, and we as a society have decided that the best way to do that is to sit across from someone and ask how many siblings they have.

The "spark," too, is a lie. This is well-trod territory, but butterflies and sparks are often a sign that you've identified someone in the immediate vicinity who's your type on paper and they're giving you attention. That's it! It's why one of the best rules of dating is "It's a yes until it's a no," meaning that until you're absolutely sure you don't want to date this person, it's still worth continuing to be open to getting to know them. That way, you're not relying on your existing biases—exacerbated by algorithms—to guide you on the kinds of people you should be dating, and you're spending more time getting to know people for who they really are.

The takeaway? Give the people you're "eh" on one more shot, especially if they're not your usual type. Just one. You certainly don't owe them your hand in marriage, but sometimes people have a hard time being their full selves on a first date. We often get in our own way, or are unable to get an accurate portrait of the person sitting across from us. That discomfort takes time to shrug off, and most of us deserve a second chance to connect.

In the beginning stages of dating my now-husband, Luke, I'd thought he was fun but fundamentally unserious. Like me, he was a journalist, but a freelance one, so he didn't work regular hours and stayed up insanely late playing video games every night. He was a huge flirt and a bit of a gossip, and even though I am also both of those things, I immediately declared him your average Bushwick fuckboy, a guy who's a good time but one who only needed to exist in my life "for now." (Bushwick, for those unaware, is a neighborhood in Brooklyn generally used as a cultural punching bag for insufferable hipsters.) Without really knowing him at all, I assumed that he'd been on a million dates just like ours, and that he treated every woman the way he treated me: with puppylike zeal and obvious interest. And I assumed that, just like the others, he'd drop me for someone new to get excited about in a few weeks.

Our second date was either a total disaster or a great success, depending on your definition. I'd just come from a very boozy birthday dinner and invited him to the dive bar where we gathered with some friends. Needless to say, we ended up making out in a different bar's bathroom followed by an Uber back to his place. On my way back home in the vulgar hours of the morning, slightly embarrassed by what had just occurred and therefore determined to keep all of it in the rearview mirror, I decided that I would execute my go-to breakup maneuver: not texting and hoping they don't either ("mutual ghosting," as I like to call it—more on that later).

Luke, however, had other plans. He texted me two days later, basically being like, "Hey, I like you, we should keep hanging out," as if he knew exactly what was going on in my mind. It was also the moment where I realized that perhaps I wasn't dealing with a fuckboy after all. If he hadn't sent that text and I hadn't gotten over

MYSELF

myself and decided to trust him the tiniest bit, I never would have seen him again.

I wish I could say I immediately let go of all those fears of Luke being just another excitable man-child living off the Myrtle–Wyckoff stop (a location that will be meaningless to everyone but New York women, who will have visceral reactions), but I still looked for little ways to make him prove to me that he wasn't. A direct quote from me to him in those early weeks was "I don't think you're ready for the Becca boyfriend experience" (lmao).

But underneath it all, I wasn't ready for the Becca boyfriend experience™ either. I was still stuck on the idea that I had to be with someone exactly like my type on paper. Every quality about Luke that didn't precisely fit into the romanticized ideal I'd invented was a knock against him. And that sucks! It prevented me from considering Luke as someone worth dating, which, thankfully, I got over in time. I thought finding my partner would be as convenient as a delivery service: I wanted to be able to scroll through an app and think, "Yes, that's my boyfriend," like I'm shopping for a cute pair of chunky loafers. And like a lot of daters, I was kind of an idiot when it came to knowing what was right for me, and heavily biased toward what I already knew I was comfortable with.

I do believe, however, that we are allowed to care deeply about one—just one!—superficial quality. We're humans, after all, and being a little bit bitchy and judgmental in the proper circumstances is one of life's greatest joys. Some of my friends won't date people with certain occupations—chefs and musicians are popular ones, which is insane to me (what, you don't want more *joy* in your life?), but I understand on an annoying-working-hours level. Others are inherently suspicious of anyone who calls themselves a "creative director," which is correct, or won't date people who only text in lowercase (I agree that there is something sinister about this, but some of it also has to do with our ideas about masculinity, i.e., "why do you as a man care about what your text looks like?" and really the question should be why should *anyone* care what their texts look like, but I digress).

In my own case, I've come to accept the fact that I am what some would consider a "height queen." Listen, I'm not happy about it either. But the facts don't lie, and the truth is that I've never dated a man under six feet. I've always thought it would have been a lot more romantic if Luke had been, like, five foot seven and we fell in love anyway. This chapter also would have probably had a much more poignant ending: "Guess what? Love really *does* conquer all, even our most stubborn and superficial and gendered beliefs about what men and women should look like next to each other!"

Alas, I am but a human woman, not a walking PSA on how to choose a partner in the most politically correct possible way. But remember, you only get one superficial dealbreaker. Choose wisely.

Key Takeaways:

- Think beyond your type. It's lazy, it's fake, and it's keeping you from making meaningful connections.
- When you're swiping on the apps, look beyond the photos. Read the prompts and use them to start conversations.
- Seek out a person's personality, namely whether they possess the important qualities in a relationship (kindness, stability!) versus what they provide "on paper."
- Go on the second date, and the third date. Even if the "spark" isn't there, you might be closing yourself off to a slower burn.
- (That said, you do get one really superficial dealbreaker.)

Two

CAN I PULL YOU FOR A CHAT?

Theoretically, the point of *Love Island* is to couple up with someone and convince the audience that out of all the pairings in the villa, you're the most compatible and deserving of the £50,000 prize. But I think we can all agree that the most fun-to-watch islanders aren't the ones who get together on day one and remain exclusive for fifty episodes straight. They're the ones who flirt and get to know everyone, keep their options open, couple up for a little while to see if there's a spark there, and then move on.

Nobody represents that ideal islander better than season 3's Montana, who dated no less than five guys in the house with zero apologies. Her posh-but-blunt demeanor made her sometimes intimidating to the boys in the house, but she never settled for less than exactly what she wanted.

We should all be more like Montana. Date everyone! Try people on, see what fits and what doesn't, be open to new experiences, don't settle, and keep looking until you find someone who's exactly what you've been looking for, even if you never meant to search for it. *Love Island* might have a heavily managed revolving door of people coming and going, but life can be just like that if you become the genius reality TV producer of your own dating experience. In order to do so, though, you've actually got to leave your personal villa (i.e., your bedroom) and get outside.

Of course, things aren't always as simple as when you're living in Mallorca with a bunch of conveniently hot singles. To that end, when it comes to meeting new people, we'll start with the most basic advice and work our way up to the really fun stuff. Get in losers, we're going flirting.

LEAVE YOUR HOUSE!

There are infinite ways to meet and flirt with people, but there's only one foolproof way to ensure you absolutely will *never* meet or flirt with anyone, ever: not leaving your house. I fully understand that bedrotting and scrolling through your phone is, like, the world's most satisfying activity, nestled into a secure little cocoon where nobody can hurt you. But in the same way that holing up inside protects you from getting your feelings hurt, it also destroys any opportunity for the good kind of risk, the kind that leads you to both new people and experiences that will help shape the person you'll eventually become.

This isn't to say the value of the connections we make online are less than the ones we make IRL, it just means that your world will expand a zillionfold when you turn those digital interactions into in-person ones. The next time you make what seems like a promising connection online, don't wait more than two or three days to send that "Can I buy you a coffee/drink?" text. (It's basically the normal-person version of "Can I pull you for a chat?")

If you're someone who really bristles at the prospect of getting outside and interacting with strangers, start small: Incorporate daily walks into your routine (I find it helps to do this as soon as I wake up, before I'm tempted to start scrolling). Try to catch the eye of a passerby and smile at them, or tip the barista a little extra and tell them to have a great day. Give yourself little rewards every time you make progress—an almond croissant is always great motivation.

GO TO STUFF BY YOURSELF

The next step in your journey to becoming a cool person who leaves their house with a thriving social calendar and a hot girl aura? Take yourself on dates. More than that, try to interact with at least one new person each time. You can start by bringing a book or some work to a coffee shop, then asking someone to watch your stuff while you go to the bathroom. If they seem cool, compliment their shoes or bag, or ask them if what they're reading is any good.

I'm a huge proponent of going to a bar alone. You don't have to get drunk—order a seltzer and bitters for a slightly chicer version of your standard soda water—but bars are places where more people are accustomed to approaching and being approached in public, therefore making your job a lot easier. Always sit at a barstool rather than your own table, to allow for more chances that people will come up near you to order. If you see someone you think is cute, ask if they need to check out a menu or compliment their drink. Voila! Now you're chatting.

And don't be afraid to interrupt or eavesdrop—two behaviors we're warned are rude under any circumstances but can be flirty ways to strike up a conversation. "When I started dating again after a relationship ended, I forced myself to go to bars, movies, and museums by myself, which initially felt a bit scary and lonely, but I quickly realized that solo outings are the easiest way to invite convo with someone you don't know," says my friend Sasha. "The most success I had was when I was sitting at a bar by myself, not scrolling my phone or reading a book, but rather looking around and trying to tap into my surroundings. I would listen in to people's conversations with each other, and if there was something I over-heard that I could comment on, I would try and make eye contact or smile to signify that I was listening in. In many cases I would get eye contact back, invite myself into the conversation, and somehow find myself getting a free drink out of it all!"

One time, she even reserved a seat at a cinema strategically next to someone else who seemed to be there solo by booking a spot (this only works at theaters where you can order ahead and see what other seats are already taken). "After the movie, I decided to ask him what he thought. We stayed in the theater dissecting our feelings until we got kicked out and then continued our conversation on the street corner. We ended up exchanging Instagram handles and slid into each other's DMs a few times."

TURN DATING INTO A CHALLENGE

I've been so impressed with the people I see on social media who have found a way to make using dating apps—which so often feel like either a grind or a time suck—into fun, motivating ulti-matums. Some are doing monthlong dating challenges, where each day they commit to messaging someone new, saying yes to every event they're invited to, and peppering their calendars with weekly dates and friend meetups. Some give their dating app profile to a friend and let them play matchmaker, while others decide they're going to approach someone in public every time they go out.

If you're in a city, look up any "anti-dating-app" events or sin-gles nights coming up in your area. Search Meetup or Eventbrite for parties specifically for people who are sick of the apps. Grab a friend and make a pact you'll strike up conversations with at least three new people. Like any challenge or goal, it's important to be kind to yourself if you don't stick with it perfectly, but having a goal in place can be a great way to feel like you're in control of a situation that seems like nothing but confusion and chaos.

PRACTICE FLIRTING EVERYWHERE, WITH EVERYONE

Just because someone isn't your exact type doesn't mean you can't flirt with them—in fact, I'd argue you should be flirting with basically everyone you come across. I know this sounds kind of insane and possibly a little gross, but the behaviors I'm talking about are actually extremely subtle: smiling at people, laughing easily at their jokes, asking them questions, reaffirming what they say, facing them directly or mirroring their body language, being playful and engaged. You'll notice that none of these are particularly sexual—most of the time, they're just polite social behaviors that communicate, at the very least, your interest in what they have to say, not necessarily romantic desire. Try keeping this in mind the next time you're interacting with an acquaintance, a coworker, a barista or retail worker, or anyone else you end up chatting with that week.

Then, when it comes to a situation where you *do* want to indicate a romantic interest, it's time to escalate: In addition to all of those things, add in small physical touches—a hand on a shoulder to emphasize a funny joke, a brush on a lapel to wipe away a smudge, or even pressing your ear close to their face in order to hear them better in a loud place are all ways to feel out romantic chemistry.

A key part of proper flirting technique, however, is also recognizing when someone isn't returning the vibes. If they're brushing you off, replying with single-word answers, avoiding your eye contact, or not asking any questions, don't take it personally, and move along to flirt with someone else—ideally one who'll reciprocate your energy.

BE OPEN TO PEOPLE WHO APPROACH YOU—WITHIN REASON

About half the women I know struggle with a terminal case of resting bitch face. They are, for the most part, very aware of the fact that they're constantly emitting powerful "Do not come near me" energy at all times. But if this is you, I think it's worth challenging yourself to entertain the people who are brave enough to approach you in public—at least up to an extent.

A lot of people are nostalgic for the "olden days" before dating apps, even if we never experienced that era ourselves, where meeting strangers IRL was a normal and expected part of everyday life. It's true: Dating apps created a barrier between spaces where it's acceptable to talk to strangers (aka from behind a screen, in the privacy of your own phone) and where it isn't (everywhere else). But in order to bring some of that prosocial spirit back to our lives, we have to do the uncomfortable work of extending a little bit of trust to people we don't know. We have to be polite and open and willing to hear what they have to say, and remind ourselves that the world is bigger than our own network, even if it means feeling vulnerable for a small amount of time.

Maybe for you this is as simple as turning your body toward the crowd, so that when you're out and about, you're subtly hinting that you're open to being approached. Maybe it's saying yes when a stranger wants to buy you a drink and having a short conversation with them. Maybe it's surveying a packed room instead of reflexively scrolling through your phone because you're overwhelmed.

Of course, if someone isn't being respectful (or is hammered and/or predatory), you should always feel free to excuse yourself or announce that you'd like to go back to what you were doing before, thanks. But here's the thing: You do have to start trusting people a bit. Most of them aren't out to ruin your vibe. If they breach that initial trust by being weird and creepy, that has nothing to do with you and everything to do with them. Don't let a couple bad experiences with rude idiots lead you to sour on the people that have the balls to approach strangers in public. Because it's hard!

GET CREATIVE IN YOUR APPROACH

Speaking of introducing yourself to other people, women tend to have an especially tricky time with this, considering we're often taught to be the pursued, not the pursuer. But in an era when people are simply less likely to approach you in public, sometimes you must take matters into your own hands, and maybe even get a little weird with it.

For starters, eye contact is sometimes all you need to get someone's attention. Look at them until they notice you, then break eye contact. Then try to catch their eye again, and this time, when they meet your eyes, give them a smile. If you're feeling extra bold, you can try the "come here" finger move, or just simply get up and walk over to them and ask what they're drinking/reading/up to, or what brought them there. If you're in a group, come up with a simple game to play with your friends, like a thumb wrestling tournament, and then ask a cutie nearby to join in because you "just need one more person!"

While I'd like to point out that this is *not* a pro-smoking book— smoking kills, et cetera—it is still, unfortunately, a really easy way to talk to strangers. Asking to bum a cigarette or a light from someone cute is pretty much guaranteed to grant you a window into hanging out with them for, at minimum, a few minutes. (If you don't smoke, just don't inhale all the way!) A simple "So, how's your night going?" can be the spark needed to turn a commonplace transaction into a lively back and forth.

One other idea I'm very proud of is when my friend and I were watching the New York City marathon, I convinced her to put her Instagram handle on her phone and hold it up so all the runners could see it as a cute way to get a hot runner dude to text her. I'm pretty sure she got a DM out of it, and even if it didn't lead to love, it gave the runners a good laugh.

HAVE A GO-TO CONVERSATION STARTER

In any conversation, flirty or otherwise, there will come a time when neither of you can think of something to fill the silence. This does not, in any way, spell doom for your relationship, but it's easy to catastrophize in your head while your brain's air horns are blaring "SOS! PLEASE GOD SOMEONE SAVE ME FROM THIS IMMI-NENTLY DISASTROUS INTERACTION!" That's why it's always a good idea to have a very random conversation starter in your back pocket, something that invites playful, low-pressure banter while also giving you a glimpse into the other person's psyche.

My personal go-to is one I stole from a friend many years ago: "If you were a snack, what would you be?" When asking someone this, you must also stress that this is emphatically *not* the same question as "What's your favorite snack?" Instead, it demands the other person really think about what snack food embodies their personality's purest essence, an inquiry that can actually tell you quite a bit about the person and how they see themselves. (I find that people with very high self-esteem will tend to reply with something bougie, like a cheese plate or charcuterie board, or something healthy, like a fruit salad, while self-deprecating folks will say something like microwave nachos or a half-eaten bag of Smartfood popcorn. All great answers, IMO.) An even more evocative adaptation of this question is "If you were a restaurant, what would you be?" and you can ask them to describe the location, vibe, and menu of a restaurant that best represents themselves. (The super-advanced move is to then later suggest you go on a date somewhere that fits that bill, but maybe we're getting ahead of ourselves here.)

Another solid conversation-saver I've found works particularly well on men is to ask for their "Mount Rushmore" of a certain subject. That means pick a topic—movies, cuisines, musical artists, travel destinations, whatever—and ask them to name their top four (or, in other words, which ones they'd put on their Mount Rushmore). Men, for whatever reason, seem to have a primal urge to rank the things they love and hate most. I'd be shocked if any of them resisted the chance to do so in public.

GIVE COMPLIMENTS—OR FLIRTY NEGS

It can feel like pickup artistry to "neg" someone you're trying to flirt with—that is, tease them in what you hope will be a playful way rather than an unkind one. In the 2000s, sleazy guys often bragged that by "negging" a girl, he could catch her off guard and lower her self-esteem so that she'd be more likely to take any male attention as a compliment. This kind of negging is obviously very gross and not the kind I'm talking about.

But many women say a subtle neg can be the key to being a great flirt, and that men absolutely eat it up. "I've perfected the art of being slightly mean," says my friend Sylvie. "It only works if you're feeling hot and confident, so I wouldn't try it if I rolled out of bed and was having an off day, but when you figure out what is and what isn't fine to gently make fun of, it can feel like a bit of a dance. You don't want to date someone who can't make fun of themselves and who doesn't know how to engage in banter appropriately, so I think it's a good litmus test for being explicitly flirty."

A good neg has to be something extremely superficial, of course (not like "Hey, you're ugly"): something like "You look like you enjoy board games," or "You look like the kind of guy who would be here right now." Once, my friend Lindsey told someone, "I bet you're a Joe Rogan guy," even though she was pretty sure he wasn't. "Not too long after that he was like, 'Can I kiss you?'"

There's also something to be said about taking the exact opposite approach. In addition to some light negging, Lindsey recently identified a sad development in men: She noticed that they don't usually get complimented in their day-to-day lives, especially if they only hang out with other men who worry that it'll come across as homoerotic to say a single nice thing about their friend (depressing!). So she took it upon herself to be that person. "Recently I have started complimenting men," she says. "I've seen a shift in their whole vibe afterwards. I think it works!?"

In app scenarios, usually she'll just say something like "sick stache" or "I like your cat," and it's enough for them to feel flattered. IRL, if they smell good, she'll tell them rather than trying to be coy or demure about it. In one instance, a guy on a date mentioned he'd been asked to officiate a friend's wedding, and she replied that he seemed like he'd be good at that. "He was like, 'Oh my goodness, why do you say that?!' And I said he had good energy and was good at telling stories. He then immediately started getting touchy. He took the one compliment and ran with it."

BE SHAMELESS ABOUT ASKING TO BE SET UP

When you're in the trenches of dating, it's totally acceptable to rely on your network to give you a leg up. That means asking everyone you know (and their partners and their friends) if they have anyone cute and single to hook you up with.

It doesn't have to be as straightforward as a blind date: Saying yes to every house party you're invited to, or throwing one where you ask people to specifically invite single folks, can create a more low-pressure environment to meet new people. "I've been telling my friends we should be having more house parties just to meet more people—platonically and romantically—and there seems to be a consensus that so many of us crave this return to meeting in real life rather than online dating apps," says my friend Amanda.

And if all else fails, feel free to use my most shameless approach of all, something I honestly believe every one of us should be doing: using Instagram Stories (or your social media app of choice) to set friends up.

Here's how it works: Ask a trusted friend to post a photo of you on their Story, and then write that you're single and looking to mingle, and have them invite whoever's interested to DM them. It's like a little advertisement for yourself! And even if it doesn't lead to anything serious, at the very least, you'll get an ego boost out of it. This also works in the reverse: If you see someone cute on a friend's Story, DM them and ask if they're single! If they are, ask to be set up!

I will warn you that the few times I've done this, the only people who actually reached out to my friends were the horniest people I know (or strangers I didn't know at all but who definitely had "reply guy" energy). But it's still worth trying, I think—I'm still holding out for the best matchmaking moment of all time.

THE ADVICE YOU ALREADY KNOW AND PROBABLY DON'T WANT TO HEAR FOR THE MILLIONTH TIME

I'm sincerely sorry to tell you that the number-one advice for flirting, approaching people in public, and dating in general is the one you already know by heart: Be confident. Trust me, I know how much that sucks to hear. Unfortunately, it doesn't make it not true. The best thing you can do in moments when you feel like the romantic stakes are high is to present the version of yourself who knows what they want and isn't afraid to get it. Because you genuinely deserve it. And when other people see that, they're more likely to believe it, too.

"The trick is to be so absurdly confident and high off your own supply," says my friend Laura, who is a genius at this. "I tend to make the first move, and with men it can be disarming. I think it comes down to being very decisive and not timid. Ask the question! Go for the kiss! Go back to your house to have a drink on the couch if it's going well! Light a candle!"

Now think about the version of yourself who can do all that, no problem, without doubt or fear. Think about the version of yourself who, when they get rejected—because you will, at one point or another, get rejected—decides that it's no sweat, it's simply one step closer to finding someone even better. Doesn't that sound nice?

You can be that person. You can cast a wide net, you can flirt with everything that moves, you can be shameless in your quest to date as many people as possible, you can maintain eye contact and strike up conversations even when it feels so awkward you want to be dead. Someday you will look back on this time in your life and wish you recognized how hot you were at this exact moment and took greater advantage. So, I beg you, go for it. Ask that person, in whatever way you want—say it with me—"Can I pull you for a chat?"

Key Takeaways:

- Leave your house. You're going to be hearing that a lot more in this book, because lowkey it's kind of the most important one.
- Leave your house *even if you're going out alone.* Take yourself on dates, and challenge yourself to talk to someone new every time. It can be a small interaction, but it's practice!
- Find creative ways to approach strangers, and be open to it (to an extent) when they approach you. Charisma is a muscle—you use it or you lose it!
- Flirt with absolutely everyone.
- Be shameless. Be confident. Brush it off when inevitable rejection happens, because it truly, *truly* does not matter.

Three

BECOMING THE BOMBSHELL

There's a moment in season 6 of *Love Island* US when Nicole is bracing herself to admit she has feelings for Miguel, despite the fact that she's also getting to know Kendall. The girls are in the glam room putting on foundation and eye shadow, and after the others beg Nicole to "Say it!," finally JaNa announces, "What happens in the makeup room, *really happens* in the makeup room."

Whether or not she meant to say *"stays* in the makeup room," we'll never know. But it's a truth universally acknowledged that the most sacred rituals among female friends take place when everyone's sitting around together and doing their hair and makeup. And if that's the most sacred ritual of womanhood, then the *Love Island* glam room is the damn Sistine Chapel.

Every night on *Love Island*, the cast members rinse off from a long day of sunbathing and beanbag conversations and get ready for the evening's activities. It is also, in many ways, the most entertaining part of the show. It isn't that you get to see these perfectly done-up women take their makeup off (well, it isn't *just* that). It's that the glam room is the one place it feels as though the cast members aren't aware they're being filmed. Of course they still know there are cameras following their every move, but in a getting-ready environment, there's not enough extra time or energy to care about all of that. In that moment, all that matters is making yourself look and feel as hot as humanly possible—and most importantly, doing it while surrounded by your girlfriends.

Each time the camera cuts to the glam room, it's like a scene straight out of a modern Renaissance painting: A row of women face themselves in the mirror, analyzing the work to be done. Dyson Airwraps line the "hair station"; makeup meticulously displayed from sponsored brands fills the cabinets. Racks upon racks of skintight polyblend sets from PrettyLittleThing and Boohoo are available for the taking. You can practically smell the 400-degree straighteners frying burnt hair, but it doesn't matter. This, right here, is bliss.

What's even more miraculous is the way the glam room has the ability to melt away whatever tensions are running high outside of it. Sure, the women are technically "competitors." Maybe they've got a crush on the same guy, or maybe they're jealous because one girl is their dude's type on paper. But as Liv Walker, a contestant on the same season, explained in an interview, "Someone will go at it one second, and the next second it's like, 'Oh my god, do you mind doing my winged eyeliner?'"

"Our girl group was so strong; we had each other's backs. We fight like sisters, we get ready like sisters, we share each other's clothes [and] makeup," she said. "But the best thing about having the glam room as our own little space away from the boys was that we were able to open up and be very vulnerable with each other."

You might have an era in your life when getting ready with a big group of friends was the norm. Maybe it started in middle school at your first homecoming dance when you took silly pictures in Forever 21 dresses; maybe you and your freshman-year roommate in college would raid each other's closets before every party. Maybe you've hit the jackpot and ended up as an adult living within walking distance of all your friends and can theoretically do this whenever you want.

Most of us, though, don't live in a Spanish villa with all our besties and crushes, nor do we live in neighboring Manhattan apartments like in *Friends*. But if you've ever experienced anything like it, you know that getting ready is, more often than not, the most fun part of going out, period—and that's especially true for dates. Because even if the night ends up being a bust, you can cherish the fact that you had an absolute ball of a time when you were preparing for it. You didn't "waste" an outfit, nor did you spoil a great hair day. You *created* that outfit and that hair, you fashioned a little persona and got into character for your evening.

It might sound frivolous, but when you do that, week after week, what you're doing is giving yourself the time and space to play around with fun makeup, mixing pieces, and new music. Over time, you begin to feel more and more like the "you" you want to become and show off to the world—and eventually you'll meet someone who's as obsessed with it as you are.

You don't have to be surrounded by pals to create your perfect getting-ready atmosphere. You can build a vibe in your space that elicits the same feelings as the let's-put-on-a-playlist-can-you-do-my-eyeliner feeling, on demand, whenever you want.

Here is the exact ten-step routine of how I would achieve this:

> The night before a big date (or one of those nights out when you and your friends are like, "Let's actually *meet* people tonight!"), take a bath. By "bath" I do not necessarily mean a literal bath, although that's the ideal version. I mean spend a crazy amount of time doing something that exists solely for your own pleasure and also maybe involves sitting in a delicious-smelling environment and watching reality TV shows (know any good ones?), or, if you're fancy, I dunno, listen to Bach and

read Dostoevsky. The point here is to *luxuriate*. Not in money—you do not need to spend a dollar—but in time. Put that phone on Do Not Disturb: You have nothing and no one to answer to, baby! Then spend the next several hours parading around eating snacks in a fluffy robe, trying out skincare masks you found in the back of your medicine cabinet. It is paramount that you do this the night before and not the day of, because if everyone had a bath before a scheduled date, I'm convinced no one would ever actually go on them.

On the day of the date, when anyone asks what you're doing tonight, say something like, "I have an engagement" or "I'm meeting a beau." The key is to sound like you're a seventy-year-old woman who wears fur coats and has been going out every night of the week since 1969 and probably slept with Frank Sinatra. Women like this are the pinnacle of chic. When somebody asks what they're up to later, they'd *never* groan and say, "Ugh, another Bumble date," because they know that even having a date in the first place is quite glamorous and romantic, even if it doesn't lead to actual romance. Plus, being too self-deprecating about your dating life leads people to think you're boring and exhausted, which, even if you are (aren't we all!), we don't need to go around blasting that information to anyone who asks.

When you get home from your day, pour yourself a glass of something extravagant. It does not need to be alcoholic (usually when I'm getting ready I wait to have my first real drink until I finish my eye makeup, for obvious reasons), but it should be something that makes you excited to drink it, the kind of drink you'd serve to people coming over for a tasteful dinner party. Bitters and seltzer is a great option, or anything and soda, really, especially if you put a little garnish on it. Don't have spare fresh sprigs of mint (because let's be honest, who does)? Try a salted or sugared rim, or get weird with it and go buck wild in your spice cabinet. When all else fails, even a Spindrift feels fancy if you put it in a wineglass.

While doing your makeup, turn on a YouTube playlist called something like "pop that pussy anthems" or "gay bangers." Women and gay men know the secret to a proper pregame, and it's watching music videos and talking about pop girlies from 2013 that normal people have forgotten about.

Do your hair and makeup the way you normally do it for going-out adventures, but take the long way to get there. Really *draw out* each sweep of blush or coat of mascara or hair braid. Art takes time!

Put on something that shows you've made an effort but not something you'll feel uncomfortable in. "Comfort," of course, means different things to different people, particularly when we're talking about psychic comfort versus physical comfort. I, for instance, absolutely love the sensation of wearing tights and think jeans are the devil, but for most people it's the opposite. Most of the world's cutest shoes are not the same as the most comfortable ones, but we feel cuter and therefore more comfortable in them because . . . they're cute! But I'm not here to tell you what to wear on a date. We'll have cycled through two hundred random internet microtrends by the time you read this book, so go with what you vibe with most.

FaceTime or text a picture of your finished look to a trusted loved one. That's for a second pair of eyeballs and some sartorial advice should you need it, yes, but also for them to assure you that you look fucking hot and fun and like a person anyone would be lucky to be going out with right now.

You're done with your makeup. You've put on your outfit. If you drink, now's the time for your first one. However, I do not recommend champagne for this occasion, because popping a bottle is just sad if you're not going to finish the whole thing, and you do not want to have drunk an entire bottle of champagne before a date. (There are very rare exceptions to this, which we'll get to later.)

You know that gay anthems playlist you've had on in the background? Turn it up!!!!! Consider the brief cultural moment that produced the would-be pop star Willa Ford and debate internally whether it really was, as she claims, 9/11 that torched her career.

On the way to the date, in between listening to "I Wanna Be Bad" again, think of at least one or two things you can say if there's an awkward lull. If all else fails, bring up the Willa Ford 9/11 thing.

See, now I'm jealous that I don't have a date tomorrow so I can start doing this right now. As Mindy Kaling famously wrote in *Is Everyone Hanging Out Without Me?*, "Do guys have any real idea how much time girls spend getting ready for a promising date? For my second date with Evan, I spent the afternoon getting my eyebrows waxed and my nails done, and spent a fortune at Fred Segal on a new skirt and even more time making the salespeople all weigh in on it. I honestly don't understand how people go on dates on weeknights; don't they want all that fun time before to get ready?"

Kaling isn't alone in her love of the pre-date ritual. "I looove to get ready," says Laura. "Bump some tunes, spray on three different perfumes, dance around the house with a little cocktail, put on makeup, put on a slay little outfit. Just really feeling myself until it's time to strut down the sidewalk. I like to enter the date with an air of 'you can't tell me SHIT' and be on the attack."

Of course, you don't *have* to spend hours getting ready if it isn't something you enjoy. For many of my friends, that puts way too much pressure on one particular date. But as Lydia notes: "Wear something that looks good while sitting *and* standing."

Like many women, Caroline always makes sure to send her location to someone before she leaves for a date. It can be super scary to meet up with someone who's essentially a stranger (considering the amount of true-crime podcasts and *Law & Order: SVU* episodes the average woman consumes, that's no surprise). Keeping in touch with a friend before and after a date can be a small thing that ensures some peace of mind. If you don't deliver that post-date debrief text, she'll know exactly what to do and which questions to ask.

———

Remember how I mentioned how you *usually* shouldn't drink an entire bottle of champagne before a date but how there were very rare exceptions? Here's one:

Charlotte always felt like she had "negative rizz," which is to say, experienced real social anxiety and an inability to flirt. It's why she preferred the dating app Feeld, where people are a lot more open about what they're into sexually on their profiles. "For some, the act of declaring pre-date what your intentions are might sound boring and like it would entirely negate the thrill of the date," she says. "But for people like myself with deep social anxiety, it really takes the pressure off and allows me to actually engage in normal conversation on the date without feeling nervous or like I need to pick up on cues or give off certain vibes."

So Charlotte uses a method I've done myself many times when I've needed more than the ten-step ritual I outlined above. "Ideally, I come to a date right off of getting drinks with friends," she says. "Chatting and getting loosened up by people who I know care about me and hype me up is a great way to go into a date feeling positive and upbeat."

This is all to say that getting ready for a date can be extraordinarily glamorous, it can involve you doing fancy face masks and getting a gel manicure and buying a whole new outfit or lounging in a literal bathtub of diamonds like Taylor Swift in the "Look What You Made Me Do" video. It can also be loud, it can be messy, it can be delightfully chaotic, and it can break every one of the "absolutely *do not* do this before a date" rules and still turn out wonderful in ways you never expected. What matters is that you feel ready to go out into the world and show yourself off. Find your *Love Island* glam room—a place where your only job is to look and feel great, a place where your friends are there to support you, a place where 2010s tropical house music bumps nonstop—and re-create it however you want. And then let's get cracking on.

Key Takeaways:

- You might not be living in a giant villa with all your besties, but you can still re-create that glorious "getting ready" vibe even if you're by yourself.

- Having a ritual and taking some time to enjoy yourself before a date ensures that whatever happens, the night was NOT a waste! Who cares if the person themselves was a bust? You had a blast (and looked amazing).

- When telling other people about your dates, try not to be a bummer or too self-deprecating about it. The fact that you're out there meeting new people is extremely fabulous, and everyone should be jealous of your very exciting life.

Four

"THE ICK" IS FOR BABIES

Olivia Attwood had a problem. Early in series 3 she'd coupled up with Sam, but something wasn't clicking. She found herself getting annoyed by everything he did and had zero desire to kiss, much less hook up with, him. "The amount he's irritating me is not normal," she admitted. She worried she was coming across as a bitch (to be fair, she did call him "a bit small town," which isn't the nicest descriptor in the world), and expressed doubt that perhaps her instincts were steering her in the wrong direction. "I've made a lot of horrific decisions dating-wise, so when I'm getting this feeling about Sam, this *ick*," she said, "I feel it in my gut, but my head's telling me 'No, that's just you again, because he's nice, he's predictable.'"

Little did Olivia know, she'd just set off a light bulb in the heads of daters the world over. Though the phrase has been circling in pop culture for decades (both *Ally McBeal* and *Sex and the City* reference it), it was Olivia who introduced "the ick" to the social media generation. After ending things with Sam, she elaborated on what she meant: "At the end of the day, when you're seeing a boy and you get the ick, like, it doesn't go," she said. "It's one of those things once you've caught it, it like, takes over your body, and it's just 'ick.'"

And thus, a viral phenomenon was born. "The ick" was the perfect articulation of something so many of us feel in the delicate early stages of dating: the sudden, uncomfortable sensation of realizing the person you're seeing is perhaps not as infallibly desirable as you once believed. It's a thrill of disgust you can't quite explain, like having a wonderful dream and then realizing it's just an illusion. The result? An immediate aversion to the person you're seeing, and possibly anyone else after, a giant alarm bell that screams at us to unmatch, ghost, and totally disengage from dating altogether, because what's the point when everything leaves you feeling gross?

Icks can range from the aesthetic (he wore hideous jeans) to the behavioral (he doesn't hold open doors for me) to random auditory annoyances (she has a weird laugh). In Olivia's case, it was kind of just . . . Sam's entire personality. Though she was one of the most entertaining islanders in the show's history, I have a little bone to pick with her choice of words. What she felt for Sam wasn't "the ick," because she never actually liked Sam to begin with. Her real problem, as she herself admitted, was that she actually had feelings for Chris, the new bombshell in the villa, of whom she said, "As much as he's a weirdo, he's hot." Chris being a weirdo might have been an ick for somebody else. But because Olivia genuinely liked him, she didn't care.

Icks, I'd argue, should not be dealbreakers. If they are, this means one of three things. In the first case, as was Olivia's, it's your gut's way of telling you that maybe you don't like the person that much. And that's great! Knowing when you like or don't like someone is actually much more difficult than a lot of people think—we tell ourselves we should be grateful that anyone likes us in the first place, or we convince ourselves they'll magically change into an entirely

BE THE BOMBSHELL

new person. Maybe your ick reflex was there all along, just waiting to be triggered.

In the second case, your ick is more than just an ick, and you've witnessed something in your partner that convinces you they aren't someone you should be dating. (I'd argue this isn't an ick—it's a red flag, which we'll get to in the next chapter.)

The third case is a little trickier. If you've felt the ick toward someone you actually like and then can't get over it, there's a chance you're valuing superficial qualities over important ones. Sure, maybe that's your gut telling you you're just not that into them—or maybe it's a sign you've got some maturing to do.

Because much like being a self-described picky eater, "the ick" is for babies. Getting icked out by the thought of mushrooms on your plate is no different from getting the ick if your date crosses his legs weirdly. Recently I read about someone who got the ick just because the guy gave her the thumbs-up. Like, what are we even doing here?

An overwhelming ick might also have nothing to do with the person at all. One psychologist told *Time* magazine that icks are often a symptom of avoidance, a "defense mechanism triggered when someone gets scared by a relationship that could hurt them—or change their life in big ways." Sometimes, she explains, the people you're instantly drawn to are only enticing because they're familiar, which isn't necessarily a good thing. The ick, then, could be a signal that a person is unfamiliar, or perhaps even a microcosm of your own insecurities. "Especially early on in dating, it could be a projection of shameful parts of ourselves or various insecurities that we have," she says.

Whatever the cause, ick culture has gotten completely out of control. So, to help determine whether your ick is reasonable, I've put together a list of common icks that plague the modern dater, and then I'll explain why they probably aren't that deep. (Remember, the following icks only apply if you *actually like* and enjoy spending

- 35 -

time with the person in question and are using the ick as an excuse to write them off.)

ICKS THAT ARE DUMB AND YOU JUST KIND OF HAVE TO GET OVER

THEY HAVE A BORING DATING PROFILE

It's maybe controversial, but I don't think cliché answers on a dating app bio are a red flag. It's really difficult to craft a compelling, marketable "self" online, and demanding that normal folks who just want to meet someone have, like, Don Draper–level advertising instincts is wishful thinking. Yes, we all know that loving tacos, making your dog your personality, and saying you're "just a Jim looking for my Pam" is extremely basic, but it doesn't always translate to them being boring people. If anything, they're probably playing it a little safe because, again, it's really hard to put yourself out there if you're not already used to curating a persona on the internet. I'll even go so far as to say that someone having *too* curated of a dating profile is maybe a better ick (why do you have so many professional-ass photos of yourself, and why are you writing a novel in your bio?!).

HOW TO GET OVER IT: Realize that we were never meant to date this way. The human brain isn't set up to sift through hundreds of people in the span of a few hours and be able to make sense of them all. By dismissing the ones that include anything remotely basic or boring, you're closing yourself off to a *ton* of potentially great people who are, as many a dating profile advertises, "better IRL."

THEY DON'T HAVE A BIG GROUP OF FRIENDS

This one is just mean. It's super hard to make friends as an adult. Maybe they're new to the area, or maybe they're a bit introverted. Or maybe they just haven't found their people yet, for whatever reason. There have been times in my life when I felt extremely isolated and lonely, and the idea of someone I was dating seeing that as an ick would be pretty hurtful. The more important question to ask is, how are they around your friends? Are they interested, polite, and generous in conversation? Can you spot "good friend" behaviors in their actions even if they don't have a ton of people they hang out with all the time? That's a sign that their friendlessness might be a temporary thing rather than an indictment on who they are as a person.

HOW TO GET OVER IT: Think of the most extroverted social butterfly you can possibly imagine, someone who's constantly hanging out with people and attends multiple parties every weekend night—and then think of how exhausting it would be to date that person. More seriously, though, this one could be worth talking about: Ask how they feel about the fact that they don't have a ton of friends at this exact moment, and what their friendship history is. If it's a situation where they've fallen out with everyone in their life, that might be a red flag. But if they've always been an introvert or a little socially awkward and you like them regardless, don't stress.

THEY DON'T HAVE HOBBIES

Much like not having friends, someone not having hobbies in the traditional way we think about them shouldn't be a dealbreaker. For a long time in my twenties, whenever I was asked about my hobbies I'd have to be like, "Uh, getting drinks with my friends?" And if "hobby" means "what you do in your spare time," that was the truth! What I wasn't considering is that I spent my time doing a whole lot more than just going to happy hours—it just didn't really seem like a "hobby" to me. Things like listening to music, watching movies and TV, traveling, going to the gym: These are technically hobbies! Are they particularly interesting hobbies? No! But they inform who you are as a person.

These days, it's different: I figure skate, I play board games, I'm in a knitting club, a book club, and a fiction writing club. (I've always dreamed of getting really into birdwatching, but I think that's a hobby for middle-aged me.) But those kinds of organized group activities took years to cultivate, and just because someone doesn't fill their weeks with run clubs or pottery-making classes doesn't mean they're not passionate or interesting.

THEY WEAR [INSERT ANY UNFORTUNATE FASHION ITEM OF YOUR CHOICE HERE]

I once dated a guy who wore these horrible, super-tight jeans. Imagine the tightest skinny jeans you've ever seen in your life. Now make them even tighter. These were like that. And it wasn't just one pair. *All* of his pants were that tight. It was to the point where friends of mine would be like, "Is Tight Pants coming tonight?" And I'd sheepishly respond with "Yes," knowing all too well what he'd show up wearing.

Anyway, it didn't matter, because Tight Pants was a great boyfriend. He was kind, thoughtful, and still hot despite his sartorial choices, which I chalk up to the fact that it was the 2010s and skinny jeans were still at least sort of cool.

But sometimes I hear the way people make fun of men for the way they dress and I wonder whether this is a situation where they're projecting their own insecurities about taste and class and style and everything else we associate with clothing onto this random dude who's just trying his best. It's possible that maybe he hasn't been exposed to the right influences yet, and in that case, once you're properly dating, you can make a little Pinterest board for him and then help him shop for clothes that do look good (aka what I should have done with Tight Pants). Win-win!

Looking back, I'm also a little bummed that I never brought up to my friends that I didn't love it when they made fun of his clothes. I know they were just being funny, but it was way too easy for me to let friends' opinions cloud my own. I started to believe that everyone was laughing at me behind my back (or worse, pitying me), to the point where I was less able to appreciate all the aspects of Tight Pants that weren't about his Tight Pants. Y'know, the actually important stuff.

HOW TO GET OVER IT: Stop letting other people's judgments influence how you feel about someone you're dating. Of course, you should listen to your friends if they express concern that someone is treating you poorly. But maybe don't sweat it when they make fun of their pants.

THEY'RE NOT AS CLEAN AS YOU—OR THEY'RE TOO CLEAN

This is another controversial one, but let's face it: You are never going to end up with someone who has exactly the same cleanliness habits as you do. (Anyone who has ever lived with a roommate understands this.) I've been both the messy one and the clean one in relationships, and there's no doubt about it: Being the clean one is much worse, despite the fact that when you're the messy one, you admittedly do shoulder a lot of guilt whenever your partner is cleaning and you were simply enjoying a nice night on the couch. I get it!

It can be easy for the cleaner of the two people to write off a relationship with a messy person. But this is one of those scenarios where people really can change—at least a little bit. No, they're probably never going to become a total neat freak, because not everyone's brain works like that. Tons of people can walk into what you might consider a disgusting sty and find it perfectly acceptable. What they can do is adapt their behaviors to a level you find acceptable.

Let's say you show up at their house and there's dishes in the sink, the bed isn't made, and there's no clean hand towels in the bathroom. Two of those things are annoying and arguably impolite. But one of those things directly affects your ability to feel comfortable in their space. That's the one that you have every right to bring up. It's totally fair play to say something like "Hey, when I come over, would you mind just making sure there's a clean towel for me to dry my hands off in the bathroom? It would mean a lot." If they get the message, then great! There's a likelihood that they'll be willing to take your feelings into consideration in the future. If not, it might be a sign they're unwilling to compromise. And at that point, it's not an ick. It's a red flag.

THEY'RE UNTALENTED AT A THING THEY THINK THEY'RE TALENTED AT

See, this one is kind of charming. Oh, to be someone who doesn't constantly second-guess themselves and is unafraid to pursue their dreams! I aspire to be this delusional! Having dated multiple fledgling stand-up comedians, I understand that watching someone bomb onstage is like the emotional equivalent of peeling back a particularly painful hangnail, but it doesn't mean they'll never improve. Also, life is about trying and failing and continuing to try again. Someone who embraces that is someone who understands that it doesn't always have to be so serious all the time.

"One of my exes was a really embarrassing dancer," says Charlotte. "Like he was one of those white boys that took a hip-hop dance class once and enjoyed it a little too much. I think he knew that he wasn't particularly a 'good' dancer by any means, but he really loved to dance. We'd go out—to a club, to a party, to someone's wedding—and he'd be putting on those moves, often making eye contact with me while doing it. I'm gonna be honest, it was a bit hard to stomach at times. That said, I loved him dearly, and I knew that there were definitely things I did that he wasn't so fond of either. At the end of the day, he loved to dance, and I thought, who am I to get in the way of this man letting his freak flag fly? It's been a while now, but I'm almost certain that when we broke up, I ended up missing those goofy-ass moves." See? Kinda cute!

HOW TO GET OVER IT: Breathe a sigh of relief knowing you're with an adult who's adventurous enough to try something they're not already good at. Taking risks like that is brave, and increasingly a rarity!

THEY DON'T HAVE THE "RIGHT" TASTE IN MUSIC (OR FILM, OR TV, OR BOOKS, OR WHATEVER)

As someone married to a man who is an absolute, unrepentant music snob, but whose own musical tastes are more in line with whatever the main pop girlies are putting out now, this one is quite personal. Luke used to imagine himself with someone who could chat with him endlessly about '90s indie rock and '80s post-punk; instead he ended up with someone whose top artist on Spotify Wrapped has been Taylor Swift for several years in a row (with the exception of 2024, thanks to *Brat* summer).

But as he once wrote in an article, "Projecting an entire personality on someone because of shared appreciation for New Order is a terrible, toxic thing to do. True love is so much bigger than that, but young people (especially young men) fetishize cultural paraphernalia— liking the same Aronofsky movie or whatever—as if it's a checklist to determine romantic chemistry. In reality, record collection–driven dating is the saddest, most skin-deep method to seek out human connection." He's right! Do I wish sometimes he'd get over himself and just sit and watch *Love Island* with me? Of course! Does the fact that we have different tastes spell doom for our relationship? Of course not. (Also, I promise I'm very cool and have good taste in other ways.)

> **HOW TO GET OVER IT**: Remind yourself that now *you* get to be the one to introduce them to all the cool stuff you love. And also that people who are way into having the "right" taste are both boring and cowardly. Stand for something! Even if it's objectively lame!

THEY'RE "TOO FEMININE" OR "TOO MASCULINE"

Listen, if you're icked out by someone's gender presentation or failure to perform their sex in a way that you find respectable, then you should really do some soul-searching to figure out why it bothers you so much. This goes for men who have very strong opinions on how women should dress or wear their makeup, but it also goes for women who are super turned off whenever a man expresses emotion or does something stereotypically "girly." Get out of your bubble, please: Not everyone is interested in being an "alpha man" or a tradwife.

HOW TO GET OVER IT: Join us in the twenty-first century and understand that a world in which "men act like men" and "women act like women" is one that is fundamentally unequal and oppressive. The people who are trying to sell you on this version of the world are lying to you.

ICKS THAT ARE OBJECTIVELY DUMB BUT ARE STILL LEGITIMATE REASONS TO BREAK UP WITH SOMEONE

THEY HAVE BAD BREATH

Much like how I argued that everyone is allowed one really superficial quality to hold dearly as "their type," you also get one—just one!—with the ick. Mine is bad breath. It's gross! Making out is one of the best parts of dating, and you're just okay with giving all that up? No thank you!

———

. . . And that's the end of the list.

———

I'll admit, there *is* one good use case for the ick. It's when you use it as a weapon to get over a particularly debilitating crush. I've seen women try to create scenarios in their heads that give them the ick all over the internet, where viral trends like "icks to get over your crush" offer a plethora of imaginary instances that promise to rid oneself of all sexual desire. Examples include imagining him "trying to hit a pinata and missing," "on a trampoline playing crack the egg and he's the egg," "running to catch a bus he just missed," "asking someone to take a hit of their Juul," "celebrating too early in bowling and then not getting a strike," and "failing to start a chant at a sports event." These are all objectively very funny and humiliating in quite mundane ways.

But they are all, crucially, experiences many of us have shared. (Minus the sports chanting one. I can't imagine anything more horrible.) My point here is that being a human necessitates suffering some amount of humiliation. Consider your eyebrows. Almost every woman I know either had a phase where she plucked them out until they were wispy commas sitting in perpetual surprise over her face, or she overlined them into two brick-like rectangles due to consuming way too many 2016-era makeup tutorials. We look back on those photos with shame and embarrassment now and still thought they looked cool at the time. It's only natural to cringe at your former self, but I don't think any of us should feel regret about it. In fact, if you're not icking yourself out from time to time, you're not really living.

I think people are hypersensitive to the ick these days in part because coming across as embarrassing or cringey has much higher stakes than it once did. Social media has made it so that we're constantly terrified of being filmed in a compromising situation, being ridiculed online for it, and then having that being part of our reputation forever. I often see younger people online commiserate over the fact that "nobody's having fun in the club anymore." Instead, everyone's on their phones and too afraid to let loose and dance because they worry that footage might show up on someone's Instagram Story the next day. These are reasonable fears, but you lose something even greater: You lose the fun of having truly let go, and the excitement and spontaneity of allowing yourself to be surprised.

We expect each other to curate "perfect" social media feeds that show we're having just enough fun (but not too much!), that we're gorgeous (but not a narcissist!), and that we're successful (but don't try too hard!). I think it's made us harder on each other and more likely to view the very normal parts of life that are a little bit embarrassing as something that must be optimized or snuffed out. It feels like everything we do is analyzed and mined for its social acceptability, rather than understanding that these are constantly shifting targets, and to put too much stake in them is to fail to live in the moment.

I don't mean you should settle for the just-okay messy guy with the ugly pants, no friends, and no interests, and who only watches Marvel movies (or conversely, judges you for watching *Love Island*). Getting over an ick is not the same thing as settling for someone who isn't right for you. What I mean is that we're all a little embarrassing, and in order to be in a relationship with someone else, you've got to compromise just the littlest bit on your ideal person: the guy who dresses like a rom-com lead, who's effortlessly calm and collected no matter the situation, is a natural at everything he tries, shares not only the exact same standards of cleanliness as you do, but the same taste in music and film, too. That guy doesn't exist, because that guy was written in the imagination of an author or screenwriter (who is probably a woman).

Any normal person will give you the ick at some point or another. And guess what? That also means you'll give someone else the ick, too. Even Olivia Attwood, a *Love Island* hall-of-fame ick-haver, understands this. Speaking about her current husband, she said, "Brad and I give each other the ick all the time. Like if I'm in a restaurant, the other day it happened, I went, 'Excuse me' to a waitress and she didn't hear me, and he went, 'Oh my god, this is an ick.'" If the Queen of Icks can get over hers, you can, too.

Key Takeaways:

- Icks, by their nature, are superficial. If you get an overwhelming ick sensation that you just can't get over, it's probably a sign that you don't like the person that much, and it's your body's way of telling you they aren't the right one for you.

- If you *do* really like them and you still get the ick, try to put it into perspective. Maybe what you're really worrying about are other people's judgments, your own projections, or some stubborn beliefs that aren't serving you anymore.

- All humans are going to be a little embarrassing at some point or another, even you. Pretty much anyone you end up dating is going to give you the ick in the future—you just kinda have to get over it.

Five

ALL MOUTH

Maura Higgins had countless iconic moments during her time in the villa, but perhaps none more so than when she overheard her then-partner Tom talking about her in front of the other boys. It's one of the most intense exchanges I've ever seen on *Love Island*, but it's also what made her so loveable and relatable to women everywhere.

Here's what went down: Maura and Tom had been chosen to visit the Hideaway, a separate bedroom in the villa designated for couples selected by either the public or the other islanders when they feel a couple deserves it. It's the spot where, historically, many of the contestants have hooked up for the first time, not just because it's decked out with sex toys and condoms but because it's mercifully shielded from the prying eyes of their fellow contestants, who normally all have to sleep in the same room together.

Maura and Tom are both thrilled, obviously—until Maura

overhears Tom cavorting with the other boys. After Tommy Fury hands him a condom, Tom remarks, "It'll be interesting to see if she's all mouth or not," referring to whether Maura would hook up with him, since she would sometimes talk and joke freely about sex. "Did you actually just say that?" she asks as her face begins to fall. "Wow," she says as she walks away. "That's a dickhead comment."

Every woman who's ever gotten her hopes up about someone only to discover they're more interested in, say, having a laugh with the lads than speaking about their partner with more dignity understood how she was feeling in that moment. Which means it was also extraordinarily cathartic to watch Maura call out Tom for being a "follower" for going along with the boys' jokes, and for her to ultimately declare that "I don't want a lad, I want a gentleman."

Imagine if she hadn't heard that comment! Perhaps she might have continued dating him for much longer in the villa, only finding out he'd said anything on the fateful "movie night" episode when past clips are aired to all the islanders. Or perhaps by the time she fully realized the maturity level he was at, they'd have been together for so long that she'd feel like she couldn't break up with him. (For anyone wondering: It's literally *never* too late to end it with someone you're no longer into.)

As disappointing as it must have been to overhear, Maura is lucky that it only took a few days in the villa for Tom to show his true colors. And it's also lucky that when Tom showed her who he was, she believed him, and reacted accordingly by ending the relationship.

Remember how we talked about how icks shouldn't be dealbreakers? Here are the things that actually are. Red flags, dealbreakers, whatever you want to call them—they're a sign that the person you're with isn't the person you hoped they'd be. Sometimes they're glaringly obvious, other times it takes an objective outsider to show you that you may be ever so slightly colorblind.

To be clear, just because you get a red flag from someone doesn't necessarily mean they're a terrible person, or that they don't deserve love or happiness. All it means is that they aren't right for you specifically. And just like Maura did, when people show you who they are, believe them.

So let's commence with our parade of flaming red flags, which come in a stunning array of light pinks to moody maroons to cherry crimsons. Red is a beautiful color—but on a flag, it's always best observed while running far, far away.

THEY'RE RUDE TO [INSERT ANY GROUP OF PEOPLE AND/OR ANIMALS]

My best friend's mom used to tell her to watch out for how men treat cats, because that's the true testament of their character. Cats, more than most animals in general, because they're the kind of pets that don't give their affection freely to just anyone. They come and go as they please and are incapable of being micromanaged. This isn't to suggest that all dog people are evil control freaks in sadomasochistic relationships with their pets (although plenty of people on the internet have indeed argued this), but rather that to love a cat is to understand that ultimately you can't force it to do anything it doesn't want to. If it wants to lie around all day, it will do that. If it wants to hide in the corner, it'll find crevices in your house you never knew existed. If it wants to yowl every morning at sunrise for its wet food like my cat does, it will continue to do so until you just sort of have to accept that your new wake-up time is the break of dawn.

A good partner will do the same for you. But they'll also do the same for anyone else they come across, including people who are often at the receiving end of such insolence: waiters, bartenders, bank tellers, retail staff, delivery drivers, cashiers, janitors, and low-wage workers in general. If you're out with someone and they're straight-up mean to a server? Honestly, I'd walk out right there and leave them with the tab. (Just make sure your server gets a big tip.)

It should go without saying that this also applies to any other group of people, be it their race, gender, sexuality, religion, disability, or weight. The thing about bigots is that eventually their bigotry will be turned against you. It's only a matter of when.

THEY DON'T ASK QUESTIONS

It's one thing to be so nervous on a first date that you contract a terminal case of yapper's disease, only to realize your date hasn't gotten a word in since you ordered the drinks. It's another to fail to take any notice of the other person and fail to express literally any interest in them whatsoever.

It's wild to me that "men not asking questions on dates" has been such a talked-about red flag, and that there are *still* men out there who haven't gotten the message. I say if you encounter this in the wild, feel free to jut in with your own opinion and say something like "I know you didn't ask, but here's what I think," or "Do you have any questions for me?" Either they'll get it or they won't.

THEY DON'T RESPECT YOUR INTERESTS

My friend Sasha's personal dealbreaker is people who hate astrology, and in particular, people who go out of their way to dunk on it. "Something about me is that I will be bringing it up any chance I get and if you roll your eyes we have no business together," she explains. Astrology is one of those things that men in particular tend to denigrate as fake or a waste of time, but whatever your personal views on it, if the person you're dating is rude to you about something you're interested in, that's a sign they're likely to be dismissive about more serious matters, too.

THEY'RE WAYYYY TOO INTO APPEARANCES

A certain amount of pride in oneself is healthy. But someone who's clearly so obsessed with coming off a particular way that it reeks of desperation is a major red flag, not least because chances are they're judging you just as much, if not more, than they're judging themselves. "I can tell right away when someone's putting on a front and acting macho and being a loud idiot," says Tiana. "When a guy is putting on, and by that I mean when they go on and on about a thing that makes them look like a big guy, most often it does the exact opposite," adds Liza.

It's a problem with self-described "alpha" dudes, of course, but there are even less obvious examples of this. Men who are extremely careful to present a highly curated version of themselves to the world are often more concerned with *seeming* like the kind of guy women want to date, and believe that alone is enough. Worse, any man who's too into appearances is significantly more likely to be judgmental of *your* appearance and only want to date someone whom they feel improves their own status. Translation? He considers you an object, and will treat you accordingly.

This also isn't just a thing to watch out for with dudes. My friend Andrew says that one of his red flags for women is "anyone expecting me to spend a certain amount of money on them or people who turn up their nose at, like, a dive bar that I suggest and want an expensive cocktail bar." In those instances, he says, they usually end up being rude or materialistic in general.

THEY'RE CONSTANTLY GETTING DRUNK OR USING DRUGS AROUND YOU

It's common for young people (and that includes folks in their thirties) to enjoy partying or a wild night out. But if someone is always drunk or high in your presence and that bothers you, you're allowed to bring it up. Don't sweep this kind of stuff under the rug, whether there's an underlying substance abuse problem or not. Talk to them about it, and suss out whether there's a bigger compatibility issue there.

THEY REPEATEDLY TELL YOU THEY'RE "NOT LOOKING FOR ANYTHING SERIOUS"

I'm of the possibly controversial opinion that, in the very beginning stages of a relationship, it's perfectly normal to tell someone that you're only looking for something casual or that you're not ready to get serious yet. Especially when you're in your twenties and early thirties, that's actually a pretty healthy way to go about dating, and I tend to get suspicious of people who want to supercharge a relationship way too early on (more on this in the next chapter!).

However, if you've been seeing someone for more than a few months and you're interested in dating them exclusively, and they repeatedly have told you they just want to keep things casual (or if you're already in an exclusive relationship with them and they tell you they don't want the same things as you do), what they're really saying is that they'll be okay if you dump them. And you don't want to be with someone who won't be devastated to not have you in their life.

People who are a little bit cowardly tend to do this. They give hints that it probably isn't going to work out with you long term (a) so that they can say they did and (b) because a part of them hopes they don't have to be the one to end things. They want you to dump them. And in that sense, they're right. You should!

In other words: Take people at their word. Know yourself and your limits well enough to understand that a "no" can sometimes be subtle. They've shown you what they're willing to do, and that might not always meet your expectations. Don't take it personally, and move on to someone who's on the same page.

THEY HAVE NO PASSIONS OR AMBITION

As we discussed in chapter 4, just because someone doesn't have hobbies doesn't mean they're a worthless, uninteresting dud. But to not care about anything at all and have zero desires whatsoever? I don't even necessarily just mean about career and money aspirations here. I mean literally anything that motivates you to get out of bed, whether that's a pet, a daily walk, a meetup with a friend, hell, an iced oat milk latte. It's okay to be passionate about silly things, but to not be passionate about *anything*? What a boring way to live!

THEY'RE JEALOUS OR CONTROLLING

We all get jealous sometimes, but the biggest sign that someone's jealousy is a problem is when it's used as a weapon. Maybe the goal is to punish you for something, or to gaslight you into believing a series of events that flatters their perspective, or maybe it's to cut you off from your support system.

The latter in particular can have devastating consequences, writes clinical psychologist Andrea Bonior. Isolation, she says, "raises the risk of abuse exponentially, as the controlled person is less able to have others in their life help them see how unhealthy their relationship is and less able to get support in escaping. Jealousy is most definitely problematic when it is used as an excuse to isolate someone ('You know I can't stand it when you go out with your friends, because they talk with other guys and you don't need to be talking to any other guys but me. They're not good for you. You need to stay home.')."

You might think this could never happen to you, that you value your friends and family too much to ever let someone else get in the way of that. But that's what everyone thinks before they find themselves stuck in a relationship like this. Jealousy and controlling behaviors are the first warning sign toward far more serious abusive behaviors down the line. The first time you get the sense you're being manipulated, it's time to evaluate the person's behaviors and talk with a trusted friend or therapist about what to do next.

THEY LIE

Maybe it's just about little stuff, like their favorite film or what they like to do on weekends. Or maybe they're straight-up lying about more serious stuff, like having unprotected sex with other people. Either way, I don't think there's a ton of wiggle room here. If you're dating someone who lies to you about one thing, chances are they're lying to you about a lot of things.

Unless, I suppose, we're talking about men's heights. Somehow that one gets a pass, if only because pretty much every man in the entire world would be guilty.

THEY HAVE TOXIC RELATIONSHIPS WITH SEEMINGLY EVERYONE IN THEIR LIFE

We've all been in toxic relationships, whether with a friend, a family member, a roommate, or a past partner. But when you're listening to someone's laundry list of complaints about the people in their life, it's worth asking what—and who—the common denominator is.

THEY SHIT-TALK THEIR EX

Ditto times two for this one. Having a shitty ex is a tale as old as time, but that doesn't mean you need to carry that negativity with you into your next relationship. Plus, you're only getting one side of the story. Constantly shit-talking your ex is a sign that either you're not over the person, you're holding a grudge, you've got an anger problem, or you're trying to subconsciously tell the person in front of you what not to do in a relationship. There's a way to do that, and it's called "being normal and communicating directly."

THEY PUSH YOU TO DO THINGS IN BED
YOU DON'T WANT TO DO

If someone pressures you to do something sexually that you're not absolutely 100 percent into, do yourself a favor and either have a very serious discussion and ensure they fully understand your side and are sorry about it, or dump them immediately. Sexual trauma sticks with you way longer than you think, and it's not worth jeopardizing your happiness and safety just so that you can please some random person who clearly doesn't care about your boundaries. Accept that it isn't your fault, and move on with people who get it.

THEY'RE MOODY OR ANGRY ALL THE TIME

As a Cancer, far be it from me to criticize someone for their moodiness. But I think in most cases, there can only be one crab in a relationship. When there's two of you, the times when you're both in good moods are so few and far between that the relationship becomes more about soothing each other's spiky emotions and "giving each other space" and less about actually enjoying your time together. I've been in relationships like this, and I eventually realized it was over when we'd make plans to hang out and I'd be overcome with anxiety over what kind of mood he'd be in when I arrived. Because chances are it was a bad one, and it'd be my job to bear the brunt of it.

THEY OVERUSE THERAPY-SPEAK

This is another slightly controversial one, but I find people who lean heavily on therapy-speak to be *really* difficult to have honest, loving, and fun relationships with. That's because these phrases are often tools that people use in order to get away with ultimately being selfish.

By "therapy-speak," I'm talking about the incorrect use of psychology jargon that's meant for specific contexts but is widely misused, usually as a way to legitimize the person's feelings. Phrases like "holding space" and "setting a boundary" have been helpful for many people to articulate their needs and speak up for themselves. They can be extremely useful to help detach from our emotions and communicate clearly with others. They can also be used as weapons.

Trying to control what your partner wears, who they hang out with, and what they post online is not the same thing as setting a boundary. When you refer to every heightened emotional interaction as "triggering" or "trauma," you're conflating conflict with abusive behaviors. These terms are often used not to accurately describe situations but simply to shut down an argument and for one side to feel like they've won.

THEY'RE EMBARRASSED OF YOU

Are they only ever texting you late at night? Do they often talk about their friends but never want to bring you around them? Do they constantly post on social media but somehow never about you? These are potential signs that, for whatever reason, they're ashamed or embarrassed of you. Believe me when I say this has absolutely nothing to do with you and everything to do with their own shame and self-esteem issues. Which, sure, sucks for them. But that's their problem to work out, not yours.

THEY'RE "BAD AT TEXTING"

I saved this one for last, because come on. Seriously, we're still doing this, after two decades of smartphones? People aren't "bad at texting," they're simply unwilling to put in the absolute bare minimum to make a plan to see you. Explains Luke, my go-to source for decoding Man Brain: "If a guy is into you, they'll make an effort to text you back."

But honestly, it's crazy that this even requires decoding. Sometimes it really is that simple.

Alas, we've made it to the end of the red-flag parade! Once again, I think it's important to reiterate that just because you're dating someone who's a little bit of a walking red flag doesn't mean that person is inherently evil. It just means that's your gut telling you they're not right *for you*.

It's also worth noting that Tom eventually apologizes to Maura for making the sexist joke, who in turn gives him credit for not lying to her about it. They end things on good terms, even though they're no longer together. It's a great lesson in navigating the trickier parts of dating, the parts where what you imagined in your head no longer lines up with the person in front of you. That part sucks, obviously, but just like Maura, you're better off knowing sooner than later. Speak up for yourself, end things kindly, and move along. On to the next!

Key Takeaways:

- When people show you who they are, believe them. If someone isn't kind to you, never communicates or texts back, is always moody, talks shit about everyone they know, and doesn't seem interested in you, your life, or your interests, they're not going to magically change in the future.

- Extreme jealousy and controlling behavior early on in a relationship is a huge red flag. The first time you get the sense they're keeping tabs on you or trying to isolate you from other people, bring it up to them, and discuss the situation with a close friend or therapist. Same goes if they overuse therapy-speak or you suspect they're using it as a manipulation tactic.

- Just because you get a red flag from someone doesn't mean they're a bad person, or that they don't deserve love. It just means they're not your person.

- Nobody is actually "bad at texting"!

Six

DOING THE MOST

It's always very cute and romantic when, against all odds, a couple decides to make it official in the *Love Island* villa. But it's especially exciting when they do so in a way that's more than just one person asking the other a simple question (not to mention makes for much better TV). And nobody did it as over-the-top as Luke did when he asked Siânnise to be his girlfriend in season 6 of *Love Island* UK.

Siânnise, who famously was obsessed with Disney princesses, was shocked when, seemingly out of nowhere, another islander presented her with a bejeweled paper crown. He then led her on a treasure hunt throughout the villa while their fellow contestants peppered her with rhyming questions about her and Luke's time there. Finally, they led her to the top floor, where Luke was waiting on a daybed, with sparkly gems on his face to match her crown. "Obviously, you've been a big part of my journey in the villa, and I want to show my intent outside the villa," he said. "So I want to ask you if you want to be my girlfriend."

Fans squealed along on Twitter/X, where they dubbed it one of the cutest moments in *Love Island* history (even though the whole thing was, for whatever reason, set to a creepily slowed-down piano cover of Hall & Oates's "You Make My Dreams"). And they're right! It was adorable, not least because it incorporated her own interests and acted as a walk down memory lane for their relationship.

Depending on your tolerance for sentimentality, Luke's treasure hunt could read either as a lesson in how to be a perfect gentleman who knows his partner inside and out—or as sickeningly sweet schmaltz designed to make him look like a star. (Some might even see it as an ick.) Whatever your opinion, it probably says a lot about whether you're the kind of person who values grand gestures or finds them a little suspicious.

Maybe it's a big, over-the-top surprise party with everyone you've ever met, maybe it's sending a flash mob to your workplace. Maybe it's a spur-of-the-moment, all-expenses-paid vacation, or maybe it's a handwritten poem. Maybe the person in question has watched one too many '80s teen rom-coms and showed up with a boom box outside your window. Hell, maybe it's skywriting (do people still do this?). A grand gesture can be any of those things and a million more. And just like there are a million ways to do it, there are also a million things those grand gestures can mean—not all of them necessarily good either.

At the risk of sounding like the world's biggest killjoy, I'll just come out and admit the thing you've probably already guessed: I think a lot of this stuff is extremely overrated. That's not because I don't love love (what else are we even doing here!) but because I often find that doing a grand gesture for someone else puts an undue pressure on that person to react exactly as expected. You become an object of attention, unwillingly on display, and if you don't perform well, you're looked upon as ungrateful, undeserving, suspect. Suddenly you're floating above yourself, staring down at someone else who was just going through the motions.

I don't know about you, but I *really* dislike being put on the spot. Before my husband proposed, I had to drill it into his head that I absolutely, under no circumstances, wanted anyone around to witness it. Not our family or friends, not a photographer, and certainly not random strangers on the street or at a restaurant. Part of that was fear that I wouldn't react the way women are "supposed" to—that is, gasp and cry, but in a pretty way—and the other part of it was wanting to have something just for us, without the pressure of having to perform for the public.

Thankfully, he listened, and even though that means our "engagement story" isn't all that exciting (we were sitting on the couch, in our living room), I so appreciated that he took my wishes into account, mostly so that I will never have to look at a photo of whatever my face was deciding to do in that moment, which was almost certainly not pretty.

I'm not alone. As my friend Haley notes, "I feel like ego is often involved in grand gestures and it's more for the person doing it rather than who it's for." I can't help but agree, particularly when the person doing the grand gesture really wants everyone to know they were the brains behind it. "I think smaller, more consistent actions are more meaningful," adds Sarah. "Grand gestures are the other side of the coin to ultimatums—big shifts in behavior to compensate for something."

Nearly everyone I asked mentioned that grand gestures are great in theory, but often a little tricky in practice, especially when you're in the early stages of dating. "I think grand gestures are great—if they are not being used for manipulation or to excuse bad behavior," says Desiree.

Then there are the grand gestures that could even be considered a little sinister. My friend Clara recalls that the only time she'd received a grand gesture, it was from an ex who later became abusive, and he'd taken her on a holiday to Portugal. Looking back, she says, "It's usually a sign of love bombing to me."

You've almost certainly heard of this concept, even if you've never experienced it firsthand. Love bombing is a popular term for when one person lavishes the other with attention, promises, and, of course, grand gestures, but without the follow-through that truly makes a relationship strong. People who love bomb will often tell the other person exactly what they want to hear, even if they likely don't know each other well enough for it to be meaningful. As one psychologist explained to *The New York Times*, "It's part of the idea of excess and overwhelming the person so that they're swept off their feet," and that the "constant attention, flattery, seduction, gifts" make it difficult "to process that you're overwhelmed. And when you're overwhelmed, you don't see danger."

People who love bomb may also want to see themselves through the eyes of their prospective partner—as a romantic hero, perfectly attuned to the other's needs so that the other person never has a desire to see anyone else. Remember how we talked about jealousy red flags? This is the exact same thing in a different flavor. In other words, it's manipulative and controlling, so much so that the term originated with cult leaders in the 1970s, who used "constant affirmation, hand-holding, and prolonged eye contact" to recruit new members.

Or, to put it in *Love Island* terms, it's what Aaron did to Kaylor on season 6 of *Love Island* US. That was according to Kaylor in the season's reunion episode, who called out Aaron for lying to her during their time in the villa about what he did while in Casa Amor. "Quit love bombing me. I cannot believe I wasted my entire fucking summer on you, Aaron," she said.

When love bombing becomes a problem is when someone makes big promises at first, then acts like you're crazy to expect them to actually mean what they say. I remember going on two dates with a guy whom I had a freakish amount in common with—we had connections to the same places, read the same writers, shared the same opinions—so I believed it when he made little references to the dates we'd go on in the future, that one day he'd be showing me around his hometown. The two times we went out, he'd be effusive and touchy-feely, but then when I texted him to make plans a few days later, he became evasive and standoffish and eventually stopped responding altogether. We didn't use the term "love bombing" back then, but I remembered questioning what he was getting out of that, considering we never even hooked up: Did he just enjoy feeling like the kind of person who could, at least for a brief period, be that perfect boyfriend? Or did he genuinely think we were going to seriously date, only to change his mind? It's infuriating that it's not always possible to know.

There's a fine line between love bombing and just being a dude who got swept up in the idea of a person (or perhaps the idea of being the ideal partner), only to realize that the person in question is, well, an actual *person* and not just a concept. And who among us can't relate to that? Anyone who's ever had a crush on someone just because they listened to cool music or dressed in a way we thought was cute has experienced this. Like all pop psychology terms (think "gaslight," "trauma," and "narcissist"), "love bombing" can easily be used to pathologize behaviors that are ultimately normal, even if they hurt someone or cause harm. They're often overused to the point of meaning nothing at all: If sending a few texts in a row to your crush is "love bombing," then wouldn't we all be guilty?

Sylvie says that her now-husband began writing her monthly letters five years ago when they were long-distance, but continues to this day even though they live together. "The gestures I received always seemed to come in the written form," she says. "I've had poems written for me in the covers of books and songs written about me and I've been written into novels. All very romantic." She's also returned the favor: "My love language is gifting, so likewise I have also written poems as gifts. I've traveled across the country to show up for people and declared my love dramatically. Sometimes, especially as a woman, I am worried about being branded as crazy or over-the-top," she says, but ultimately, she thinks the idea of grand gestures is a severely underrated one.

This is an extraordinary example of a grand gesture that's a genuine reflection of the strength of a relationship. The grand gesture also required effort and was a way of expressing sincere feelings. I don't want to pretend I'm immune to a heartfelt letter or a word-vomity display of affection: One of the relationships I look back on most fondly was founded on a tradition of writing each other long, lovely letters when we lived across an ocean from each other. I didn't post about these letters. They were for me! And I cherished them. There's no gesture grander than the thoughtful, sentimental ones.

I think that's why I've always been so skeptical of the sort of people who parade their grand gestures—either those they've given or those they've received—online. This stuff makes for really engaging social media content, to the point that it almost seems like the entire goal of the gesture in the first place was to brag about it. One convenient way to show that you've won at life, after all, is to show all your followers that you've got someone who will constantly buy you flowers, take you on fancy vacations, and spoil you with expensive gifts. But when it starts to become a competitive display of over-the-top actions to outdo others, then it starts feeling a lot more cynical.

That's what you've got to watch out for in the beginning stages of a relationship, when you're letting your mind race with all the cute activities you're going to do together in the months ahead, when you're sending adorable good-night and good-morning texts, when you're showing up with little gifts that show you remembered something they mentioned about loving a certain band or wanting to try a particularly delicious-looking pastry they saw in the bakery window the other day. Sometimes, when you feel carried away, it's worth asking: Are we both on the same ride? And is it a ride I want to be on?

What's more important than impressive gestures are the little things—everyday things that show that your partner cares. It's not the performative pronouncements, nor the big bouquet of roses for social media, it's the calling and texting to ask how your day went, it's the planning the date, it's the remembering that your brother recently broke his foot and asking if he's doing okay. Those are the things that make for a happy, fulfilling relationship.

When in doubt, talk to a trusted source, the kind of pal who won't shy away from bringing you back down to earth and coaxing you to maybe hop off the ride for a while. It doesn't mean you can never get back on again, or that there will never be another one you'll take a spin on. It just means that perhaps this ride is going a little too fast for you. They just don't want to see you get sick and swear off amusement parks forever.

Key Takeaways:

- We all have different love languages, but grand gestures like big gifts or over-the-top surprises shouldn't be a replacement for the more foundational aspects of a good relationship: trust, communication, honesty, and joy.
- Watch out for love bombing (when someone peppers you with attention, promises, praise, and gifts, then doesn't follow through or pulls away).
- In many cases of love bombing, however, it's a situation where the person had an idea of you in their head and then couldn't handle it when they realized you're an actual person and not just a concept. As much as it really sucks to be on the receiving end of this treatment, it's just a sign they're not the right person for you. Good riddance!
- Dating someone who asks about your day and who's invested in your life and your feelings is much more valuable in the long run than someone who surprises you with a grand gesture every once in a while.

Seven

YOUR PERSON WILL TREAT YOU LIKE A PERSON

Contestants on *Love Island* are almost never shown discussing what goes on in the outside world—with the magnificent exception of that time Hayley asked if the English county of Essex was a continent. So in series 3, when Jonny and Camilla, one of the most intelligent and poised women to ever appear on the show, strike up a conversation about who would pay on a date, which then led to a debate on feminism, it came as a huge surprise, both for audiences unaccustomed to political topics on the show and for those under the assumption that Jonny was a decent guy.

Here's how it went down: When Jonny tells Camilla he didn't let his previous girlfriend of five years pay for a single shared expense, she's curious about why. "Surely at the beginning it's better to go halves, because you don't know how it's going to pan out?" she asks him. He then replies that he'd feel "emasculated" if a woman paid on a date. Observing her shock, he smirks and says, "You're a feminist, aren't you?"

"Shouldn't we all be feminists? Surely you believe in equality?"

she asks. He then argues that, actually, he thinks feminism has gone too far, and that women have already achieved equality in the UK. Camilla, as usual, handled the interaction that followed with far more grace and generosity than I would have. She understands that the most persuasive arguments are delivered calmly, reasonably, and kindly, and goes on to explain that because the systems in which we live have been set up generations ago for men to be the sole breadwinners of families, we're still dealing with the consequences of the patriarchy.

Unfortunately, like too many conversations around feminism, the man in this case did not come out of the encounter with an appreciation of the new perspective Camilla graciously offered him. Instead, Camilla ends up in tears, scolding herself for falling for Jonny too quickly before she fully had the time to recognize the way he views the world.

If you've ever been on a date that sounds like this, congratulations, you are eligible for financial compensation. Just kidding. But I do genuinely believe there should be some sort of fund for the emotional damages experienced by women forced to explain Feminism 101 to random Tinder dates. The problem is that if such a fund did exist, it would deplete immediately.

That men and women have fundamentally different experiences of the world is one of the great tragedies of heterosexuality. You can meet a guy, really enjoy spending time with him, even fall in love with him, and still, he can say something that reminds you that ultimately he will never know nor will he fully empathize with what it's like to be a woman. And no matter how hard you try to break it down, there's still a cognitive dissonance at play.

We're in an extremely polarized political moment. Increasingly, men and women are diverging in their beliefs, with women drifting more to the left and men to the right. That shift is particularly pronounced in young people. Since Trump's election in 2016, the percentage of eighteen- to thirty-year-old single women who identify as liberal has climbed from 20 percent to 32 percent, while young single men moved several points to the right. It isn't just the US: Around the world in places like South Korea, the UK, and Germany, men and women are splitting their votes based on gender, with the youngest voters diverging the most.

This could constitute a major crisis: What will it mean for dating if the sexes can't even agree on the most basic political principles? Some, like *The Washington Post* editorial board, have suggested that "about one in five young singles will have little choice but to marry someone outside their ideological tribe" and that "*someone* will need to compromise."

It doesn't take a genius to work out which "someones" they're talking about. The implication is that women will just have to figure out a way to settle for men who disagree with them politically if they ever hope to get married.

For women, these topics aren't just fun, abstract tit-for-tat arguments to have over a beer. The women lurching to the left are doing so in part because our immediate personal safety is at risk with certain political parties in power, parties who pass draconian abortion bans that end up killing women or letting them die because doctors fear they'll be imprisoned if they perform life-saving care. The effects of politics aren't just theoretical. It's about the system viewing us as human beings who are capable of making choices about our own bodies.

Which means that there are about to be a whole lot more first-date blunders like Jonny and Camilla's. I don't think that's necessarily a bad thing. In fact, it could be a *great* thing. More people should get comfortable with discussing their morals and belief systems relatively early on in a relationship. Just because someone you're dating doesn't share your exact perspective and experiences—which would be both impossible and boring—doesn't mean that person is inherently wrong or bad. Being challenged is part of what dating entails: You try people out and see how well they fit, while also remaining open to how you yourself could evolve, too. Camilla learned that she doesn't fit with Jonny, and that was a gift!

But there's one quality that's an absolute nonnegotiable: Your person, if they're really "your person," will treat you like a person. That means they'll care for you in ways that aren't simply transactional, and they'll make an effort to understand your needs. They'll take your desires seriously, because they *are* serious. Your person will trust that you are capable of forming your own opinions and knowing what's best for yourself. Your person won't seek to control your beliefs or behaviors, because they'll view you as a whole, real person, just like themselves.

To that end, you're perfectly capable of figuring out the line between your opinions and your morals. Once you understand the difference between more surface-level beliefs and the kind that come from a deep-seated and immovable sense of right and wrong, it's a lot easier to see whether you're compatible as people. When you decide what you both truly value, the smaller differences are easier to work through, using your intuition as the guide.

As we touched on in chapter 3, this is especially pertinent when you're taking safety precautions before meeting up with someone for the first time. When you're going on a date with someone from the apps, you should be following basic guidelines for safety, and anyone you're dating should be understanding of the fact that meeting up with a stranger can be frightening and you've got to look out for yourself.

THAT MEANS:

- Pick a public place to meet. Don't go to a stranger's home before you've met them, and don't invite them to your place—even if it's only for a hookup. Meet at the Starbucks around the corner if you have to.

- Always have an exit strategy. Sometimes that means arriving at the location early and paying for your first drink in cash; that way if you need to leave at any point, you don't have to wait to pay your tab. It could also involve you limiting yourself to a certain number of drinks so that you'll be okay to get home no matter what. Most importantly, be sure you're not relying on the other person for transportation.

- Search their name and any other information you have about them online. Check out their social media profiles to see if there are any red flags or if they match up with how they present themselves on an app.

- Wait to exchange phone numbers until you've met them in person and you decide you like them. Keep your communication limited to the dating app until then—first, because it protects your phone from having one hundred contacts called "Josh from Hinge," and if they become a problem, you can turn to the platform for help. Plus, without your phone number they won't have access to as much other information about you.

- Share your location with a friend, or at least text someone you trust about where you'll be (and remember to follow up when you get home!).

- Recruit the bartender (or barista, or whatever professional staff are around) if you need help. If you arrive early, let them know you're meeting someone for the first time and you're a little nervous, and they'll be sure to keep an eye out. If you feel uncomfortable or unsafe, let them know.

- Don't bring a first date to a place you frequent all the time (and if you do end up at such a place, don't tell them you're always there). Not only does this prevent awkward run-ins in the future, but if things go really sour, you don't want them showing up looking for you.

- Remind yourself it's always better to be rude and safe than polite and hurt.

You'll notice there's no hard-and-fast rule about how long you should be talking to someone before you actually meet up with them. That's because people go through phases where they like to be *really* selective with their time and will only see someone IRL they feel is super promising, and other times they've caught the social butterfly bug and are ready to bop around with whoever's available. Both are great! Neither is better than the other. Sure, a long get-to-know-you video call is a great way to screen a potential date before you go through the effort of seeing them face-to-face, but it's impossible to tell whether that chemistry will translate to real life. On the other hand, speedrunning dates can be fun, but it also could be a way to give yourself dating burnout (and we all know burnout is for work, not your love life).

Regardless of which category you're in at the moment, pay attention to how the person you're dating is treating the boundaries you've set. When you tell them that you don't need another drink, do they try to push you to order one anyway? When you insist on calling yourself an Uber versus getting in the car with them for a ride home, do they mock you for being "paranoid"? When you say you had a great time but you're not interested in seeing them anymore—or that you don't want to do [insert any sexual act]—do they get defensive and lash out?

There are even less serious examples we could use here: If you're dating someone and they're consistently not checking in on you after you mentioned you appreciate a good-morning text, or if they don't remember personal details about you (as in, the basics of what's going on in your life, not, like, your grandmother's maiden name), and you mention that fact to them in a "hey, what's up with that?" sort of way, do they think you're being super extra or too demanding?

All of these responses are signs that this person isn't really considering you a real person with your own valid wants and needs—instead, they see you as someone who owes them something just for being in their presence. (Spoiler: You don't.) It can be super scary to reject someone when you're not sure how they'll take it, but the best way to do so is by being both polite and firm.

Like most things, understanding your own boundaries and determining what you're willing to compromise on is a whole lot easier in theory than in practice. Sometimes you can date someone for a while before you sense something's off. For Sasha, she realized it wouldn't work when he refused to kiss her after she'd gone down on him because he thought it was "gross." "I unfortunately internalized a lot of his hatred of women and thought that it was something unique about me that he hated," she says, echoing an all-too-common sentiment. "We dated for a few painful months until one night I lost my shit and screamed at him in a public restaurant and walked out. Thankfully, that was the last time I saw him even though he tries to slide into the DMs to this day." (Classic.)

This kind of stuff can be really tricky to predict from the outset—

you can enjoy getting to know someone, and suddenly something they do can totally throw you off and change how you see them altogether. It's almost like a much stronger version of "the ick," where you're not quite sure what it means or how you feel about it, and it takes a few days (or weeks or months) to process it.

I've found that the only way to know what to do in these situations is by bringing it up and seeing how the other person reacts. I know it's tempting to try to solve every prodding issue or question you have by poring over it in your head or discussing it in painstaking detail with friends, but unfortunately, the only real answers you're going to get will come from the person themselves. Otherwise you're just circling around the problem, not addressing it head-on.

Let's say, for instance, you had an awkward moment during a hookup that left you spiraling about a small comment that might mean one thing but might also mean something else entirely. Instead of driving yourself crazy with guesswork, bring it up directly and see how he reacts. You can do so in the moment if you feel comfortable enough, or you can wait until the next time you see each other, in case your feelings evolve. Say something like "Hey, when you said this during XYZ, it stuck with me, and I'm wondering what you meant by that." If he's reassuring, respectful, and willing to talk things through, that's a sign that he's viewing you as a whole person with her own feelings and boundaries. If he's flippant and defensive, maybe it's time to reevaluate.

Just because your political opinions or ideas about how dating should work aren't perfectly aligned doesn't mean a relationship is totally dead on arrival. But the bottom line is that you owe it to each other to treat each other like human beings. And if you get the sense you're not being treated like a grown-ass person, get up and use your big-girl legs to walk very, very far away.

Key Takeaways:

- Don't be afraid to bring up your beliefs—political, moral, spiritual, whatever is most important to you—in the first couple of dates. Even if the person doesn't share your exact perspective and experiences (no one person could!) doesn't mean they're wrong or bad. But at the absolute bare minimum, they need to respect your perspective.
- Keep in mind certain safety basics before heading out on a first date. Pick a public place, have an exit strategy, share your location with a friend, and don't bring your date somewhere you go all the time.
- If someone you're dating says something that concerns you, or alerts you to a potentially serious mismatch of beliefs, bring it up. How they react will tell you a ton about who they are.

Eight

TO SHAG, OR NOT TO SHAG

On the very first season of *Love Island* in 2015, Hannah and Jon "christened the house," and the show was never the same. Though they'd first done it when they visited the Hideaway together, it wasn't until weeks later, when they hooked up in the bedroom in full view of their fellow contestants, that the tone was truly set: *Love Island* is a show where people get it on with not only the cameras watching, but their housemates, too.

In possibly the funniest scene of the inaugural season, the moment Hannah climbs on top of Jon and throws the comforter around them both, the *Jaws* theme starts playing. They begin to have sex in a way that is so hilariously obvious—both visually and audibly—that the other islanders start to notice and laugh, while Hannah pokes her head out from the covers and turns around, grinning, to see if anyone's paying attention. When another islander makes a joke, Jon cries out, "I can't stop now, guys, you just have to deal with it!" then later says, "Lauren, please, you'll make me lose a boner here!"

After they finish, one guy complains that he could "fucking hear that through earplugs," while Jon covers his penis and gets up to use the bathroom, but not before playfully mooning the cast. The episode then cuts to a live stream of host Caroline Flack, who announces that it's "the most disgusting thing I've seen on the show so far." It's also one of the best.

From Hannah and Jon's public bang sesh to season 2's Olivia and Alex, who claimed to have had sex thirty times in the villa despite the fact that Alex hadn't even been in the house for a full thirty days (producers allegedly had to keep refreshing the condom supply every morning), sex has always been the raison d'être of *Love Island*. Season 3's Montana apparently spent a full twenty minutes on top of Alex, while the previous season's Terry and Emma-Jane had sex above the covers in full view of their housemates, assuming incorrectly that the footage wouldn't be shown. (This led to several complaints to the UK's communications regulation bureau, though the show was ultimately cleared.)

You'd be forgiven for assuming that this also means that sex is a total free-for-all in the villa, but there are strict rules for anyone who engages in it. Each couple who has sex must meet with a counselor afterward, and drunk sex is not permitted, as contestants are limited to two drinks per day. Masturbation, too, is forbidden, even in the shower (though naturally, many of the contestants have found ways around this rule). Condoms are sprinkled everywhere, a not-so-subtle urging by the producers on behalf of safe sex.

This isn't how it works in the real world. There's nobody waiting behind the scenes to ensure you haven't had too much to drink, distribute free condoms, or set up a meeting with a professional psychologist after a one-night stand. Yet it's worth asking: Would real-life sex be better if it was just a little bit more like it is on *Love Island*? I don't mean everyone should be doing it in front of their friends or refraining from some self-love time. But perhaps the sex people are having would be even better if we borrowed some of the conventions on the show.

For example, you might not need an individual therapy appointment after every time you have sex, but checking in with yourself before, during, and after doing the deed can be crucially important to ensuring that it's a fun and worthwhile experience. Sometimes the best way to do that is with a professional, but other times all you need is a gabfest with a trusted friend or a juicy journal entry. Being mindful of how much alcohol you've consumed is also a really good way of being certain that (a) you actually want to be having the sex you're having, and (b) you'll be fully present—and therefore more likely to enjoy yourself—during it.

In the meantime, there are plenty of other pillars of great sex to keep in mind before getting it on that ensure you'll have the best time possible and remain true to yourself while doing so. We'll start with one of *Love Island*'s most iconic slang terms.

FOLLOW THE FANNY FLUTTERS

If there were a polar opposite phenomenon to "the ick," it would be "fanny flutters," another *Love Island*–ism popularized by Maura Higgins. (This was when she first met Tommy Fury and said, "I'm having fanny flutters, I'm not even joking. I wish he was eating me.") I assume I don't have to explain what this means—its American counterpart would be the phrase "vagina dancing," and you've either felt it or you haven't. The best example I can give you is it's that feeling you get when Mr. Darcy in the 2005 adaptation of *Pride & Prejudice* walks really slowly through the field in his little trousers and tells Keira Knightley, "You have bewitched me, body and soul, and I love, I love, I love you." They are, in other words, your body's way of telling you that you want someone, in this case a fictional Regency-era man written by a woman.

Whatever you want to call that particular sensation, it's more than just a fun little quirk that happens to our bodies; it's a useful signal to understand whether you actually want to hook up with someone or if you're doing it for the million other reasons people have sex: because they're lonely, because they're bored, because they're afraid to say no, because they're scared of disappointing the other person, because they want to gain more experience. Fanny flutters, or the other ways our bodies tell us we're turned on—like an elevated pulse or a fiery sensation in your skin—are evidence that not only do you want to be having sex, but that you're ready for it in the moment.

This is not to say that fanny flutters are logical. You might find yourself feeling them in the weirdest possible circumstances, situations where you absolutely should *not* be having sex. To use a similar example as the above, it's like when you were a kid and you watched the Disney version of *Robin Hood*, the one where he's a fox (in more ways than one). In that case, it does not mean you are attracted to foxes or that you should be having sex at all, it just means you're a human with a healthy libido.

NAVIGATE THE ART OF THE HOOKUP

So, you're nearing the end of a date at your local bar, waiting for the check, and you're debating whether you want to invite them over to your place. Chances are that means the date went reasonably well, you're attracted to the other person (perhaps you even had a flutter or two), and it's time to decide what to do next.

First things first: Don't invite them over until you've kissed. Whether you go in for it when you're sitting down or wait until after you've left, a make-out session, even a short one, will tell you whether you're interested in anything more.

Second, make sure that you trust them enough to bring them to your home (and therefore let them know where you live). The benefit to hosting rather than going to their place is that you don't have to figure out how you're going to get home afterward, although of course, if the person invites you over, the upside is that you can leave whenever you want. Neither is correct—it depends on what you're most comfortable with!

Third, just because you end up at one of your places doesn't mean you have to have sex, or do anything else, for that matter. But I do find it to be a nice gesture to set the tone. Have a vibey playlist or a record ready to go, light a candle, and turn on your moodiest lamp (never the big light, dear God!). If you must, or if you're extremely nervous about the prospect of making pre-hookup conversation, you can turn on a show or a movie, although I think this can sometimes feel a bit high school. If you were already chatting on the date, challenge yourself to keep the conversation going at your place. Much more chic!

DON'T FEEL AWKWARD ABOUT BEING AWKWARD

Tragically, having sex with someone for the first time won't always feel like a beautifully smutty scene in a romantasy novel—instead, it can be like two monkeys trying to ballroom dance. Good on the monkeys for trying, but there's always room for improvement. Chances are the very first time will be just a little bit weird, and the good news is that it doesn't spell doom for your sex life going forward.

Sex therapists recommend talking out some of your anxieties with your partner before going at it, taking things slow (meaning:

lengthy foreplay!), and sharing what's worked for you in the past if something isn't working in the moment. A simple "I like it when you XYZ" or, conversely, "I don't like it when you XYZ" goes a long way, especially if it's your first time with that person. Keep in mind it's probably not that person's first rodeo with awkward sex either, and it happens to the best of us.

PRACTICE SAYING NO

Here is your friendly, always relevant reminder that you are well within your rights to say no at any time before or during sex if you realize you're not enjoying yourself. Or for literally any other reason. That's it. Full stop.

This is especially important considering we're in an age where practices like choking are increasingly common, even without consent. Choking is a perfectly fine kink to have if that's your thing, but it's not okay to inflict it on someone without asking first. One study found that 58 percent of female college students have been choked during sex, and that women will often go along with it not because they're particularly interested in being strangled, but because they think it turns men on.

Many women are scared of coming across as prudish or "vanilla" if they're not gung ho about the kind of sex that's common in porn, where men often develop their sense of what "normal" sex entails. The problem is that a lot of the most popular pornography features sex where women are choked, hit, verbally degraded, or otherwise humiliated. Again, these kinds of kinks aren't inherently wrong or bad, and pornography itself is not inherently evil when it's produced ethically. But that doesn't mean it's your job to be fulfilling men's pornographic fantasies every time you have sex with them. Porn is entertainment, not reality, and it's not like men are out here embodying all of women's biggest sexual desires. (If they were, there'd be a lot more Mr. Darcys on these streets, and I'm not seeing any.)

INSIST ON SAFE SEX

"The amount of adult men who refuse to use condoms these days is staggering," warns Lydia. "They may not outright say it, but they say they cannot maintain performance with one on, which is essentially the same thing. An excuse I hear a lot is that they didn't have to wear one in their long-term relationship."

Though younger people are having less sex in general, a disturbing trend has grown among those who do: men refusing to wear condoms. Experts point to the medical advancements made in both birth control and STI drugs, as well as the lack of comprehensive sex education in schools, as reasons for this shift. "I've had friends who go home with a guy and say they're not having sex unless they use a condom, and immediately the reaction is either a reluctant, 'Okay, fine,' or 'If you don't trust me, then I shouldn't even be here,'" one college student told CBS. "They're like, 'Well, I'm not dirty, so why would I use them?'"

This kind of manipulative behavior—not to mention the deeply stigmatizing labels of "dirty" and "clean" when referring to STI status—is extremely not okay. It sets the expectation that women are there to cater to men's preferences, just so that men can enjoy the maximum amount of sensation during sex even though it puts both parties at risk. Ignore every people-pleasing bone in your body and insist on condoms anyway. Say something like "Unless we use a condom, we're not having sex." If they respect this boundary and are understanding, great! If not, fuck them (and not in the fun way). Anyone who takes one off without your consent is committing a form of sexual violence that is punishable by law in certain countries.

Meanwhile, you should also be getting tested regularly. "I try to get an STD test once a quarter if not after any new partners—trust no one with your own health! Even if you're in a committed monogamous relationship!" Lydia adds.

TRY TO AVOID DRUNK SEX

Much like how the contestants on *Love Island* are limited to two drinks per day, I think that's a decent guideline for having sex. I'm not saying drunk sex is inherently bad or predatory, it's just almost always better when you're present in your body, and alcohol robs you of that experience.

As a fan of alcohol generally, I understand that sex is a lot easier to have when you're drinking—you lose some of those pesky inhibitions that stop you from approaching someone in public, telling them you're interested, or inviting them back to your place. It helps rid your brain of those things you tell yourself that get in the way of having meaningful sexual experiences: that you're not good nor beautiful enough for anyone to desire, that your naked body will somehow be a disappointment to the person looking at it. I get it! Alcohol can be great for shooing away your anxiety and self-consciousness and make it so that your "yeses" in the bedroom are loud and confident as opposed to awkward and meek.

It can also, however, lead you to make some harmful decisions you wouldn't have made otherwise. There is quite possibly nothing worse than waking up in a place you don't recognize next to a person you don't know and having no recollection of what happened the night before. Alcohol is often the reason people cheat, the reason they have sex without protection, or the reason they sleep with people they know they shouldn't. As fun as it is to have a few drinks on a night out, if you're past the two- or three-drink mark and are on your way to blacking out, maybe stop, have a glass of water, check in with a friend, and rethink whether this is something you really want to be doing. After all, what's the good of having sex when you won't even remember it?

EMBRACE THE HOOKUP BUDDY

"Friends with benefits" sometimes gets a bad reputation in pop culture, but in the right circumstances, I think it can solve two problems at once. The first problem is, obviously, that you're horny and want to be having sex with someone. And the second problem is that you don't have to go fishing in the dating pool to find a person to do that with—instead, you want someone reliable that you can trust, someone who knows you and your body and is very much on the same page about what's happening here.

In this way, I think having a friends-with-benefits situation (which is emphatically *not* the same thing as a situationship, wherein one person refuses to commit to the other and won't refer to it as an actual relationship) can raise your standards of what you'll accept into your dating life. When you already have your trusty hookup buddy to fool around with on the regular, you're less likely to settle for someone who isn't kind to you or who otherwise fails to meet your standards. You can also often feel freer to be yourself and ask for what you want without judgment (both in and out of the bedroom), because the stakes are lower than in a romantic, monogamous partnership. This person isn't supposed to be "everything" to you; they're there to have fun with. Plus, if you already know the person, you're able to skip through all that awkward, stilted first-date chatter ("So, what do you like to do on the weekends?") and get right to the good stuff.

The key is to always keep things super straightforward and honest with your buddy. If one or both of you are having sex with other people at the same time, you should be getting STI tested regularly. If one of you starts having feelings, then it's time to reevaluate the parameters of the relationship. Until then, enjoy it while it lasts. A great hookup buddy is a precious resource! Savor that shit.

AND IF YOU WANT, UPGRADE TO A ROSTER

The next step up from a hookup buddy? *Multiple* hookup buddies. Sometimes one person can be really great for satisfying certain needs (or maybe they're really good at a specific bedroom activity) and others are fun in other ways. Building your roster—that is, people you're dating or hooking up with simultaneously—can expose you to whole new worlds of sex and new facets of your sexuality you didn't know existed.

Of course, it also means you need to be extra clear with everyone that they're part of a team, per se. Assure all the people on your bench that you're practicing safe sex, and make clear they should do the same with their own roster.

WHEN YOUR FANNY FLUTTERS END IN SHAME

If your fanny flutters do end up leading you astray, if you end up hooking up with someone you were super attracted to and they turn out to be a shitty person, do not, under any circumstances, blame yourself for it. One of the most difficult parts of a one-night stand is the guilt that lingers afterward. Even though, culturally, hooking up with a stranger and never seeing them again isn't seen as a huge deal anymore, many of us might have complicated feelings about the sex afterward and still deal with deep shame about it.

Maybe you realized later that you felt a little used or unfulfilled by the encounter, and you have every right to feel that way. Try working through it by shifting your perspective: People have sex for all kinds of reasons, and not every time will be as meaningful as you'd like it to be. That has zero bearing on the kinds of sex you'll have in the future. You are not defined by your sexual experiences, whatever they are!

Moreover, it's important to remind yourself that you were doing what felt right at the time, and hopefully you had a blast. Remain open to encounters you think could be fun, but if they don't work out exactly the way you intended, do yourself a favor and go easy on yourself. Even the strongest, wisest woman can follow her fanny flutters too close to the sun. But I bet she had a great time on the way up.

TUNE OUT OTHER PEOPLE'S JUDGMENT

People's sex lives, particularly women's, are going to be critiqued no matter what. If you are having it, you're either having too much of it or with too many people, you're doing it too early or at too young of an age, you're "giving away your power" or you're "ran through." And if you're not having it, you're a prude, or an incel, or, if you happen to be reading any one of the thousand think pieces about this, a victim of society's loneliness crisis.

Many people will tell you their own rules for having sex, and that's cool for them! It doesn't mean you need to follow suit, nor should you feel obliged to. Much of the time those rules don't even really work the way people think they do. "I've tried doing the 'wait X number of dates before we sleep together.' It never matters," says Lindsey.

"I think that if anyone is that concerned with the 'rules' around sex, there's a bigger issue at play—and they're not the person for me anyway," adds Meredith.

I personally can't stand the somehow-always-prevalent discourse around a person's "body count," or the number of sexual partners they've had in their lifetime. It makes women feel shame if our "count" is high, and it makes us feel shame if it's low, thus putting pressure on us to raise it. *Love Island* US even made a whole game out of it in season 6, where contestants had to guess how many people their fellow islanders had slept with, as well as voice their own opinions on how many "bodies" they thought were too many for the opposite gender. One dude claimed that he'd had sex with 150 women, but then answered that he believed a woman shouldn't sleep with more than ten people. Thankfully, he was called out by the women on the show, and was dumped from the island not long after. (A similar situation happened on *Love Island* Australia in season 6— seriously, what is wrong with men?!)

Placing value on someone's body count is an unwinnable game, and it is deeply dehumanizing. The kinds of people who care about that stuff will probably just find another reason to make you feel worthless, because, really, that's what it's about: judging a woman based on superficial qualities because they feel threatened by her sexual freedom. Conversely, many women often feel pressured to raise their body count in order to appease such sexual standards. Either way, anyone who asks you what your "body count" is doesn't deserve to hear the answer.

I'll say it again: Stop being so hard on yourself! Whether you've had sex with a hundred people or zero, once again, your value is not determined by your sexual history. I find that the guilt we inflict on ourselves for having sex (or not having it) can often cause far more harm than the act itself. Be kind when you're talking to yourself, and keep in mind that sex is a normal, wonderful part of life, and your decision to take part in it or not is nobody's business but yours. You can choose to reframe your sexual encounters however you'd like by taking pleasure into your own hands and viewing sex as a sacred, personal practice.

There are no cameras or fellow islanders watching you do it on top of your sheets in the communal bedroom. You are the only person you need to be worried about pleasing. So go out there and have as much silly, messy fun (responsibly!) as you can. You've only got one life. Might as well get off on it.

Key Takeaways:

- Adapt the rules of sex on *Love Island* to your own life: Always use condoms, avoid drunk sex, and check in with yourself before, during, and after every hookup.
- Let your fanny flutters be your guide, and don't be too hard on yourself if they lead you astray.
- Embrace the hookup buddy. Find a friends-with-benefits situation (or two or three), and cherish it!
- Be firm with your no. You are allowed to say no if they refuse to wear a condom, if they start choking you out of nowhere, or for literally any other reason, at any time.
- People are going to judge women for their sex lives no matter what, but ultimately, your sex life is nobody's business but yours.
- Check in with your body regularly—hot girls with active sex lives get tested every few months!

Nine

I'VE GOT A TEXT (AND IT SAYS, "YOUR PHONE IS LYING TO YOU")

At this point, it's a cliché to remark on the fact that a large percentage of *Love Island* contestants are already famous influencers or, at the very least, aspire to be. The show's been hugely popular for a decade: Of *course* its stars become social media celebrities. Islanders know exactly what they're doing when they sign up; they know that even if they don't walk away with the love of their lives, they'll walk away with hundreds of thousands or, if they're really lucky, a couple million followers. Who needs a partner when the whole world loves you?

But not one among the parade of wannabes compares to the influencer to end all influencers, Molly-Mae Hague, known best for her enormous hair buns, blindingly white veneers, and penchant for neon-green clothing (to be fair, it was 2019). After placing second in series 5 of *Love Island* UK, Molly-Mae and pro boxer Tommy Fury pivoted to being the franchise's biggest social media couple of all time, documenting the next few years of their lives as bona fide celebrities. Immediately after filming, the two bought an apartment, and Molly-Mae would go on to launch a series of beauty and fashion brands before buying a new home in 2022. In January 2023, she gave birth to a baby girl named Bambi (!). That summer, Tommy proposed on a cliffside in Ibiza.

One year later, however, Molly-Mae announced their breakup on Instagram. "Never in a million years did I ever think I'd have to write this," she said. "After five years of being together I never imagined our story would end, especially not this way." Months later, Molly-Mae's Instagram posts were swarmed with comments from fans, excoriating her ex for destroying what they believed, based on their view from the outside, to be a perfect relationship.

Here is the part where I'm going to tell you something you already know: that social media is fake, that the vast majority of people's profiles are little more than a highlight reel, that you're only ever going to see one highly curated perspective of someone's life, and that one highly curated perspective is going to be the one they want you to see. Usually where this ends up leaving you feeling is that you're the only person in the entire world who's ever felt sad (and if you are sad, you're not doing it in the sexy, aestheticized way all the cool kids are doing it online, or that you should be turning your sadness into something greater than itself: a sad-hot crying selfie, a viral breakup song, the next great American screenplay). I know you know this. Everyone knows this. It's boring to know this.

But it still somehow never fails to surprise folks when they find out that perhaps the supposedly perfect couples they see online are actually just . . . normal human relationships. Molly-Mae Hague and Tommy Fury didn't amass millions of followers by being soulmates, they did it because both of them are exceptionally skilled at portraying themselves in exactly the light they'd like to be shown in. This, to be fair, is a very valuable skill, but it is often a misleading one. Even if all of the people in picturesque relationships on social media were just as happy as they seem, it's still a performance.

When you consume tons of this content and outsource your role models, your views on what counts as an aspirational relationship become skewed. You start to place value on qualities that look good from the outside, and begin to think you'll never be complete without a partner who acts the same as the partners on social media. And when you start looking for partners from a place of deep insecurity, your judgment isn't your own anymore.

You've probably seen the many seemingly perfect couples preen over each other online, slow dancing in their living rooms, cuddling in bed, or, in some cases, extensively describing their outfits and how hot the other looks. There's nothing *wrong* with this per se—love is great! We all love love!—but by offering this performance up for public consumption, it turns love into yet another marketable display. These creators know precisely what their audience will find most engaging and envy-inducing, and continue to post more of it. And listen, it's completely normal to feel envy when you're single, but it's important to realize that your phone is lying to you, too.

Internalizing such expectations for both ourselves and others ultimately feeds into anxiety-driven behaviors that can appear early in the dating stage, especially when you're getting to know the person over text. Texts are pretty much where all of modern dating takes place, from before we even meet for the first time to years down the road when you're firing off those "need anything from the store?" messages multiple times a day. No two people text the same way, but I'd argue that the way you communicate on the phone sets the vibe for everything that follows.

Maybe you're one of those people who only like to text functionally—that is, to hammer out basic details like the time and place of your next meeting and nothing else, because the thought of spending even one more second of your life looking at your phone makes you want to vomit. Maybe you're one of those people who types in all lowercase and doesn't mind triple texting because you want your messages to reflect the quick back-and-forth banter of a high-energy conversation. The best conversationalists will adopt some of their partner's habits, like a tennis match where it takes a few sets to feel out the rhythm.

But in general, I think there are a few hard-and-fast rules: Don't overuse emojis, it's weird. If you've asked a direct question and the person hasn't responded in twenty-four hours, they're probably not interested. Don't always be the one to text first or ask them out (or pick the place you're meeting). Don't "check in" on them for no reason more than once a day (and take note when they don't reciprocate). If you're dying to text them, have something interesting and/or funny to say before hitting send, otherwise it can come off as a little bit like you're begging them to notice you (this is especially true during their work hours). Remember that a lot of people see getting a text as kind of a burden—you are, technically, distracting them from whatever they were doing before—so don't overdo it.

Again, the most important thing is to match the other person's energy: Are they being super flirty and responding within five seconds? Let those fingers fly. Are they using perfect punctuation and taking hours to get back to you? Run! (Just kidding. People are allowed to do this. Just maybe think twice before responding immediately. You've got important things to do, too!)

So much of that early texting stage of dating feels like you're just waiting around for the other person to respond. Spend too much time fixating on when and how they'll text back and you're pretty much careening toward a complete mental breakdown, however. I know how much it sucks to be frantically checking your phone in case they watch your story or reply to a message, but literally the only solution here is to . . . not do that. Distract yourself. Turn your phone on Do Not Disturb, go for a walk, crack open a book, treat yourself, do literally anything other than mindlessly scroll and stare at your device.

Plus, it's not like you're going to find the solution to all your problems on there. Multiple studies have shown a correlation between social media use and feelings of loneliness. Meta, Instagram's parent company, hired researchers to conduct an internal study of how the app is affecting its young users and found that 32 percent of teen girls said that Instagram made them feel worse about their bodies, while many others also said that it undermined the strength of their friendships, according to a *Wall Street Journal* investigation. Worse, teens feel like they spend too much time on Instagram and wish they could log off, but feel like they have to "be present" on the app, even when they know it's harmful to their mental health.

While I think telling everyone to just log off and touch grass forever is both misguided and unrealistic (social media can be a real force for good, and technology is not inherently evil!), there are ways to have a healthier relationship with the machine that makes you feel bad. The first step is to recognize when scrolling crosses into doomscrolling territory. As one psychologist explained to *Wired*, "Let's say you are feeling stressed-out at work and you disengage from your tasks to pick up your phone and doomscroll. Once you catch that compulsive behavior, check in with yourself and ask what it is you are thinking and feeling. . . . Those unpleasant feelings are there for a reason, and they communicate to us our needs, so we cannot just silence them with distractions. Once you become aware that what you actually need is support, then maybe you can reach out to a colleague and delegate some tasks."

The next step is to take a break, even if that means going back to scrolling through the stuff that *does* make your brain feel good, like, say, the r/Aww subreddit or an ASMR video on YouTube. Better yet, rather than obsessing over the lives of people you don't know or fixating on a text back, reach out to a friend. "Real-world relationships may help mitigate the negative consequences of comparing yourself to others online," suggests an article in *Self*. "They can 'make the stakes of online relationships feel less high and more balanced,'" another psychologist told the magazine.

My personal strategy for dealing with Instagram brain is my absolute favorite feature of social media: the mute button. What a perfect invention! I *love* muting people. You post something annoying? Mute! You post too much? Mute! I feel bad when I see your content because it triggers some insecurity in me I'd rather not deal with right now? MUTE, BABY! Not only is it a crucial reminder that actually you *can* be in control of the stuff that shows up on your feeds, but the best part is that they'll never know you muted them, especially if they're the kind of freak who uses one of those tools that sends a notification every time someone unfollows them (seriously, how much of a masochist do you have to be to *want* that?!). And if you're the kind of person who watches a zillion Instagram Stories in a row, you won't have to experience the jump scare of seeing your muted pal's hundredth post asking you to rate and review her podcast. There are so many people I absolutely adore IRL but whose internet presences are so insufferable that I simply have no choice but to exercise my right to *mute! that! shit!*

And yes, that includes your friends in happy relationships who post nonstop about themselves and how in love they are. The older we get, the more it feels like all those formerly single people we knew are now blissfully coupled up. Those first dates you used to commiserate about together are now solo journeys, becoming fodder to entertain your friends who are no longer in the trenches. You feel like with every new match on a dating app the stakes are higher, that time is slipping away and if you don't find a partner *right this very instant*, you'll be alone forever. It's a horribly lonely feeling, and you can be supportive of your friends' relationships without subjecting yourself to the constant reminder that they've "found their person" and you haven't.

Let me remind you: You are on your own journey, and so is everyone else. We've all got our own struggles, and if you're single and sad about it, that's okay! Know that something good is coming for you, even when it feels like nothing ever will. Maybe it's not right this very second, but trust that you will figure it out. In the meantime, get off Instagram, put your phone down, and go live your life! Go outside! Go on a date! See a friend! Do anything but sit and scroll.

This was pretty much JaNa's experience in the villa on *Love Island* season 6, who was single for the majority of her time while her pals in the "PPG" (aka the Powerpuff Girls), Leah and Serena, were connecting and having dalliances with the guys in the house. Despite the fact that she felt disappointed, she never compromised her standards for what she wanted in a man and continued to support her friends without letting any feelings of jealousy get between them. Plus, in the end, the *Love Island* gods rewarded her with a wonderful, caring, and extremely hot partner.

Anyway, if you need to mute a friend, mute a friend. It's a much healthier option than letting yourself feel bitter, talking shit behind their back, or making fun of their posts with your other pals. If they notice you're not engaging with their content anymore, be honest. A good friend will understand the need for you to maintain a social media algorithm that's free of content that makes you feel bad about yourself (I've done similar things when friends kept posting diet or fitness content and body checking).

And speaking of exercising your rights, may I also recommend making generous use of the "not interested" button? Depending on the app, it can be pretty hidden, but I can't overstate how crucial it is for your own sanity to smash that "not interested" whenever your algorithm feeds you something you know isn't helpful. It doesn't even have to be for any serious reason or particularly triggering content. It can literally just be something you're uninterested in. Maybe it's happy couples bragging about how happy they are, maybe it's that one celebrity you find infuriating, maybe it's the endless amount of weight-loss and thinspo content on your Explore page. Or maybe it's the home design influencer whose kitchen is just too perfect. If you're not interested, let the internet gods know.

After all, they're the ones who've set up this shitty system we're all in, but ultimately it's *your* screen, it's your account, and it's your phone. Most of all, it's your time being wasted on stuff that sucks. It's easy to forget that when it feels like everything in the whole world is subject to the whims of billionaires and out of our individual control, but you get to decide what you are or aren't willing to engage with online.

I should reiterate that this isn't the fault of Molly-Mae or influencers like her. All things considered, she seems like an extremely sweet person with a personal style and taste in home decor that a lot of people really admire. Being good at Instagram doesn't make you inherently fake or untrustworthy, it simply makes you a good salesperson.

And just like the rest of us, Molly-Mae struggles with the pressures of the social media comparison game. In an interview with *British Vogue* after her breakup, she wondered whether she really wanted a fairy-tale wedding with Fury for herself and her family, or whether it was part of a desire to adhere to the persona she'd built online. "Was I planning a big wedding because I wanted that image of a big wedding and the beautiful photographs and that moment that everyone would have expected from us on social media? Probably," she said.

It's funny the way social media divorces our true selves from our likenesses, the way that the real you could be living an entirely separate life from the one your Instagram portrays and nobody would be able to tell the difference. I often find myself looking back on my social media accounts from the worst years of my life and then scrolling to the best ones, and realizing that both look exactly the same. No one would possibly know what was happening off camera or how I felt about it. All they would have seen is someone smiling for a screen.

This, I think, is the most important thing to remember while undergoing the dangerous task of trying to deduce meaning from the images we consume online. Each of us is there because we want to be noticed. Every post is a plea—for attention, for admiration, for money. There is nothing more human and nothing more humiliating than this. It's okay to be single and lonely and sad about it—you can even post about it if you want! But you're under no obligation to consume everyone else's life on the internet. You've got your own to live.

Key Takeaways:

- When texting with someone, match their energy. Don't pepper them with random thoughts throughout the workday unless that's the vibe you're getting from them.
- If you find yourself freaking out over how long someone you're dating is taking to respond to you, put your phone in Do Not Disturb mode and distract yourself as best you can.
- Social media is a lie. Don't compare yourself to anyone, especially those annoyingly perfect couples (some of whom have come out of *Love Island*!) who are always bragging about how in love they are. It'll completely warp your sense of what a good relationship is.
- Almost anything is a better use of your time than sitting and scrolling on your phone!

Ten

MUGGED OFF BY THE ENTIRE WORLD

The seventh season of *Love Island* UK was made all the more delightful by Kaz Kamwi and Liberty Poole, whose giggly, fun, and clearly deep friendship convinced half the internet that the two of them should actually be crowned the winners. But between hyping each other up for dates and cuddling on the couches, they also had to deal with the more unspoken effects of being on *Love Island*: namely, the way it treats women who don't conform to the extremely narrow beauty standards set by the British television-viewing public. Though we typically think of getting "mugged off" as getting ghosted, disrespected, or otherwise made to look foolish by an individual person, sometimes the worst kind of mugging off is when it feels like it's being done to you by the entire world.

Let's be clear: Both Kaz and Liberty are absolutely gorgeous. But on *Love Island*, gorgeous isn't enough to prevent harassment from fans, microaggressions from fellow contestants, and the sensation of always being picked last. Liberty, who fit into the *Love Island* archetype of blonde with a spray tan and plump lips, received frequent social media comments about her weight. "I still get trolling where people say I've got a big tummy," she later said on Instagram.

Kaz, meanwhile, is just one of a handful of dark-skinned Black women ever to be cast on the show. And just like the few before her, Kaz wasn't picked by any of the boys on the day-one coupling. When she showed emotion, she was labeled on social media as "angry," despite the fact that white contestants who yelled at one another were called "misunderstood."

Love Island's fraught relationship with Black women has been a problem since the show's very beginnings. It took four seasons to cast a Black female contestant in the villa, and that woman, Samira Mighty, says she felt like a token among the cast. "It got to me after a while," she told the *Daily Mail*. "When you kept seeing the white, blonde bombshells coming in with these amazing bodies, big boobs, you feel like 'Oh God, another one. I'm at the back of the queue again.'"

One season later, Yewande Biala not only wasn't picked on day one, but she also faced microaggressions from one cast member who refused to call her by her name because it was supposedly too difficult to pronounce. Meanwhile, fans pointed out that she wasn't given as much airtime as the others. "We've seen nearly every Black woman on the show not being picked from lineups or ending up the last option," writes Habiba Katsha in an article for *HuffPost* titled "*Love Island* Needs Black Women. Do Black Women Need *Love Island*?" "Put simply, it's painful watching Black women being rejected time and time again. . . . For many Black girls (especially the ones who grew up in predominantly white areas), Samira's time on Love Island was a throwback to our own awkward and uncomfortable dating experiences," she writes.

As Katsha notes, what happens to Black women on *Love Island* is a microcosm of the reality of dating as a Black woman. Data has shown that dating apps and the artificial intelligence that powers them routinely exacerbate anti-Black bias and sexual racism, while the Black women using them are subject to racist messages and fetishization.

Though dating apps can be hard for anyone, they're especially so for Black women. One sociologist who interviewed dozens of people of color on dating apps found that many men "are not making the same kind of effort to engage with Black women" on the apps, where in turn Black women are "being fantasized about where they're being seen as exotic, and [white men] want to have sexual experiences with us only." Since the algorithms are already pairing people who look like one another due to outdated bias against interracial dating, that prevents Black women from being shown to a diverse set of potential matches. In other words, the apps' algorithms and people's general bias are constantly feeding off of one another, exacerbating both problems. Not only are you getting mugged off by shitty dudes on the apps, but by the faceless technology that facilitates them.

Then there are the stubborn stereotypes that make it impossible for Black women to fit into Western society's standards of femininity, which are almost always synonymous with white femininity. Sarah Adeyinka-Skold, a professor of sociology at Loyola Marymount University, wrote her dissertation on dating discrimination, and found that Black women were the only demographic of women who experience exclusion from both Black and non-Black men, who didn't want to date them because they're considered "emasculating, angry, too strong, or too independent." "Both Black and non-Black men use the stereotypes or tropes popular in our society to justify why they don't date Black women," she said. "As long as we have a society that has historical amnesia and doesn't believe that the ways in which we structured society four hundred years ago still has an impact on today, Black women are going to continue to have an issue in the dating market."

Where all this leads is that more Black women settle for less than they deserve. In an essay for *Refinery29*, Kelle Salle wrote that her experience dating as a Black woman led her to relationships that weren't healthy. "I found myself in dissatisfactory dating situations and relationships with emotionally unavailable people. I ignored red flags because I didn't want to be alone, choosing to see the potential in a person rather than who the person really was. It wasn't until my last long-term relationship ended that I realized I hadn't even given a second thought as to what I actually wanted in a partner. That didn't matter at the time because I was more concerned with not being alone. Our union was proof that I was loveable so I ignored the red flags and tried my best to make things work."

It's a familiar feeling for anyone who doesn't conform to the narrow standards set by the culture at large, including plus-size and fat women. On social media, women commiserate about "dating while fat": the fear that someone on a dating app will accuse you of catfishing if you fail to choose photos that accurately represent your size, the feeling that a partner might secretly be ashamed of dating you, and the worry, logical or not, that your friends won't believe anyone would ever actually be interested. "Lots of people are willing to sleep with fat people. Many are willing to date a fat person. Few are willing to truly embrace a fat person," wrote the author and podcaster Aubrey Gordon.

Dating, if you're a plus-size heterosexual woman, involves constantly having to consider the fragile male ego. Too many men, for instance, say they're attracted to fat women in private (or seek out and enjoy having sex with them), but won't take them on public dates out of fear they'll be judged. Bigger women are also taught, either explicitly or otherwise, that they should be grateful for whoever comes along—even when that person makes dehumanizing or otherwise hurtful comments about their body.

For this, there really is only one piece of advice you need to worry about. "The first moment you feel someone is slighting you because of your weight, your sex, your creed, your race, LEAVE them," says Tiana. "They are not your person."

For the rest of all the complicated feelings that come with dating while not fitting into our culture's most deeply held beauty norms, I think the most important thing to ask yourself is this: Why would you ever want to spend your time and the most intimate parts of your life with somebody who wishes you were different? As anyone who has lost a significant amount of weight knows, it's extremely true that people (and especially potential dates) treat you much differently, and you attract different kinds of people. But why would you want to be with those people anyway?

Even if you do fit into the beauty ideal, you're still subject to the same oppressive rhetoric. So . . . what are we actually supposed to *do* here? We know that dating is a lot more difficult for Black women, for fat women, and for pretty much everyone who doesn't look like a *Love Island* contestant (but also for them, too, somehow). And yet practically the only thing we're told in response to these reasonable feelings of rejection, humiliation, loneliness, and shame is—say it with me!—"Just be confident!"

God, I hate this advice. Not only is it completely hollow and tone-deaf, but it turns the world's problem into something your brain then has to gaslight itself into solving. As someone who has historically (and, well, currently) struggled with self-confidence, I also bristle at the assumption that the people with the most self-confidence are the ones who end up winning at life, because I don't think that's necessarily true (see: every pop star's lyrics about never feeling good enough). Plus, try looking someone in the eye who's been rejected time and time again for their weight, race, or looks and sincerely telling them that their only problem is that they're just not confident enough. Like, I'm pretty sure it's a little deeper than that, babes!

I also hate this advice because of the tiny—genuinely tiny!—part of it that's true. It'd be a lie to say that there's zero power in confidence, or that it has no effect on someone's happiness or luck. Not to sound like every toxic-positivity self-help book ever, but quite often, situations or facts of life do feel better when you choose to look at them more positively. And that can have real, tangible outcomes. As Sylvie puts it, though she's experienced ableism and fatphobia in her dating life, "If you believe you're a full catch in general, the people you are trying to date will agree with you. I never got rejected by a single man I was chirpsing because I went in with the energy of 'You wanna fuck me,' and it was almost always true. I saw so many beautiful friends of mine have a terrible time dating because they believed they were not sexy. A tragedy!"

So how do you become that kind of person who thinks "You wanna fuck me" every time you see a cutie? If there's anything that viral trends on TikTok taught me, it's this: Delusion is the solution, or "delulu is the solulu." Just as your negative self-talk can damage your self-esteem, repeatedly telling yourself *you're sexy and smart and alluring* can eventually make you believe it—and act like it. After all, what's the harm in thinking every person you go on a date with is *super* into you, that you can do or say everything wrong and they'll *still* be into you because you're just that great? If they're not, well, their loss. You can still gas yourself up about little things— the way your hair curls just so, how your eyes shimmer in dive bar lighting, your dope shoes, or how sexy your perfume smells— without turning into a narcissistic monster.

It's also the same secret to move on when you get mugged off in other ways—when you sense someone is ghosting you, or bread- crumbing you (that is, stringing you along, or when someone gives you just enough attention to keep you believing that they're inter- ested in you, but failing to show up in any real way), or otherwise rejecting you. Delulu can once again be the solulu: Perhaps that per- son had a minor brain aneurysm that temporarily caused them to see you as a wet pile of clothes, because anyone with working eyes and ears would clearly be able to tell that you're amazing and some- one no one would ever *dare* ghost. Best of all, this works in part because they're not your problem anymore, and their opinion has nothing to do with your own desirability. All their mugging off tells you is they aren't the one for you anyway.

There's another approach here, one that's radically different from the one I just described. You've probably heard of body neutrality, or the idea that your body is simply just that—a body, and not a reflection of who you are as a person or what you deserve in life. It's a necessary reminder that your appearance is not, and should not be, the most important thing about you. I think a similar approach can be taken to confidence in dating: Sure, maybe you're not the best flirt in the world, or the smartest, funniest, most fabulously dressed person anyone's ever met. But accepting that the vast majority of us will never be much more than mediocre in most respects, you're freeing yourself from the illusion that you aren't enough just as you are. It's a classic glass-half-full situation: You could understand that nothing actually matters (least of all what you look like) as a terrifying truth, or an effervescent and freeing one.

Like many of us, I tend to oscillate between three modes of thinking—that I'm the hottest, best person in the world; that I'm the ugliest, worst person in the world; and that we're all just sacks of meat trying to find some joy while we still can in the world. I find the third one to be the most life-affirming, the first one to be the most fun, and the second one to be a complete waste of my fucking time.

The thing I fear most when it comes to believing in myself—or, in the case of dating, believing that I'm desirable—is that I'll end up disappointed when, as usual, something proves that belief to be false. The problem is that when you struggle with self-esteem, you tend to see those "somethings" everywhere: That one guy who ghosted after a few messages on a dating app? It must have been because he found my Instagram and thought I was too big in some of the photos. The guy who only wanted to meet up late at night? He was too embarrassed to be seen in public with me. You get the idea. All the little "somethings" kept building into an impassable mountain of reasons why I was too fat or otherwise not good enough to love, and that discouraged me from trying at all. Instead, I waited for an imagined future when I would be thin enough or hot enough to strike up a conversation with someone and feel certain they'd like me in return.

But the truth is that there's never any certainty. People reject each other for all kinds of reasons. We reject each other for reasons we don't understand, we reject ourselves without meaning to. Having a "perfect" body or conforming to society's ideal won't save you from the all-too-human fact that no one is desirable to everyone. Life's much more manageable when you're an acquired taste.

And anyway, you're not alone here. As Liberty and Kaz's friendship showed, even if their struggles didn't look like one another's, they found solidarity and sisterhood within each other. You can build that community, too—and trust me when I say that's worth all of the romantic attention in the world.

I'm not saying you can solve prejudice and bigotry and rudeness simply by ~believing in yourself~. Nothing can do that. But a little change of perspective can grant you sanity in the meantime. And maybe, if you're like Sylvie, even get you laid.

Key Takeaways:

- When you don't conform to society's ideals about what a desirable person should look like, it can be easy to settle for less than what you deserve. Do not, by any means, fall into this trap: You deserve someone who's extremely psyched about you right now (not in the theoretical future where you might look different), and someone you're equally excited about dating.
- Everyone in the entire world is going to tell you to "just be confident!" They are, unfortunately, a little bit correct. Dating is a whole lot easier (and way more fun) when you show up to every date thinking, "They *want* me."
- Life is so much more manageable when you're an acquired taste. Nobody's for everyone—and that's the way it should be.

Eleven

MAYBE THEY SHOULD CALL IT
"FRIENDSHIP ISLAND"?

During one of his many meltdowns in season 6 of *Love Island* US, Aaron tearfully reminded everyone what the show they're on is called. "It's *Love Island*!" he shouts. "It's not fucking 'Friendship Island'!"

But Aaron, as he often seemed to be, was wrong—not technically, of course, but in essence. Anyone who's watched even a single season of *Love Island* knows that only rarely do the romantic relationships formed in the villa prove to be longer lasting than the friendships that come out of it.

Take Kaz and Liberty in season 7: Toward the end of their time in the villa, after Liberty and Jake decide to call off their relationship, Kaz tells her, "You are literally one of the strongest, most beautiful and intelligent people I've ever met in my entire life. You may not have felt like you found love in Jake, but I found love in you, and I'd like to think you found love in me."

"I found love in you!" replies Liberty. Gah!

Then there was Chris and Kem in season 3, whose friendship

remains one of the most memorable and hilarious in the show's history. They—and their notoriously tight pants—cuddled, showered together, shaved each other's initials into their pubic hair, and enjoyed spontaneously bursting into song, later releasing a grime single together that hit number fifteen on the UK charts (only real ones remember the banger that was "Little Bit Leave It").

Much like in *Love Island*, there's a very high likelihood that the relationships in your life that are the most meaningful won't be romantic ones—they'll be platonic. This goes against pretty much everything we're taught growing up: that your adult life doesn't really start until you "settle down," that your one job is to search far and wide for the person you're going to be with for the rest of your life, which ideally ends with you owning property together and, even more ideally, having kids.

That version of adulthood is hopelessly outdated, not least because owning property is increasingly an impossible dream for so many young people. Fewer of us are getting married, and those who are, are doing so later in their lives. Plus, now you have to *pay* to see everyone who likes you on dating apps. (The indignity!) You might reasonably think this would result in a golden age of friendship, with everyone simultaneously deciding to prioritize platonic bonds and create cute little utopian communities where everyone shares one giant house together. But while plenty of people have worked hard to build this reality in their own lives, we're also seeing a worsening loneliness crisis across the US.

Experts don't all agree on what's causing it, which some surveys show began around 2014 (hence, it's not all COVID's fault). It might very well be the smartphones, though again, it's likely not technology alone, rather the collapse of institutions and third places where people regularly gather. Whatever the root causes, the effects are enormously damaging. Loneliness exacerbates the risk of mental health problems like anxiety, depression, and substance abuse, while also putting us at greater risk of heart disease, cancer, stroke, dementia, and early death.

Thirty-six percent of Americans say they feel "serious loneliness," while 22 percent say they haven't made a new friend in the past five years. On average, we spend less than three hours a week with our friends, compared to six hours a week ten years ago. And we're not choosing to spend that lost time with our partners or families—we're choosing to be alone.

So where does that leave you, person who presumably doesn't want to die early and depressed? How are you even supposed to make friends as an adult anyway? Isn't finding a partner hard enough?

I find one of the biggest barriers to modern friendships are all those people who'd rather be alone on their couch than out in the world, even when they'd objectively be much better off getting outside and interacting with other people. It's not really their fault: It's literally never been more entertaining to be at home, considering anyone with a subscription to a streaming service and a cell phone now has access to basically every film, TV show, song, and audiobook that's ever existed, plus a feed of social media content algorithmically designed to keep you hooked.

I'm just as guilty of this. Despite being an unabashed extrovert, I sometimes find myself stuck in this cycle of telling myself "Meh, it probably won't be *that* fun," "it" being whatever social thing is going on that I'm too tired to attend. But more often than not, I remind myself that showing up for friends is more than just buying them a drink on their birthday and listening to them vent about their shitty bosses. It's making clear you value their time and their presence by not constantly canceling plans, and treating that after-work drink hang, however hastily organized, as sacred.

There's another trap that people fall into as an excuse to bail. In the beginning stages of a relationship, it's extremely tempting to go ghost mode on your friends and spend all your time staying in with your person, ordering delivery food, and half watching Netflix reruns. I think you get a certain amount of time where that's completely acceptable and all your friends will just have to understand that you're having the very normal and exciting experience of the hard-core honeymoon phase. But their patience will begin to wear out somewhere around the three-month mark, when they look around and realize you've been MIA for long enough that you barely have an idea of what's going on in their life. Note to all new relationship-havers: three months! That's all you get!

"When your romantic relationship is in its initial phases, it can feel like that's the most important one in your life—but keep in mind that it's new and it can change quickly, whereas your most important platonic relationships have been there for you and they continue to deserve your time, attention, and love," says Meredith. She's right! New romantic relationships can be more fragile than they feel at first, and risking your longtime friendships for some random Tinder person isn't a great look.

Sasha admits that she used to be one of those people who hopped from relationship to relationship, putting partners over friendships to "run from loneliness." "It wasn't until I started prioritizing my friends and community that I realized how much more fulfilled I was as opposed to trying to stretch one person into being my every-thing," she says.

There's a good chance that if you're reading this, however, you're in the opposite position. Maybe you're feeling like your friends have all recently begun spending way more time with their partners over their friendships, or that they've moved on from the stage of life where your friends act as your family. Maybe they're swept up in the chaos of cohabitation, wedding planning, or having kids, and seem to feel as though they can just skip out on major events in your life, sim-ply because it doesn't look like theirs. This is a *really* shitty feeling, and I'm here to tell you that, unfortunately, it doesn't really go away.

As you get older, people move. They get into relationships or really intense jobs. They have kids, they get divorced, they get laid off, they get sober. They deal with health crises or have to take care of their parents. All of these things will get in the way of being able to hang out with your besties, the way you used to feel like you were able to do all the time.

This is precisely why it's important not to put yourself in a position where you only have one or two people you can rely on at any one time. Things happen, and it's crucial for you to always be flexing your friendship muscle—that is, deepening existing relationships and putting in the effort to make new ones—even when you feel like you don't "need" anyone else.

Then there are the times where "friends" are the absolute last thing you want to hear out of someone's mouth. By this, I mean the friend zone, an experience many an islander has dealt with, even when they're coupled up. On season 7, Sharon was clearly at least a little bit interested in Hugo, with whom she was partnered on day one and then recoupled up with two weeks later. But she soon realized during a daybed heart-to-heart that he'd never see her as more than a friend. "I think it's a bit peak for me that you friend-zoned me in the first thirty minutes of meeting me," she ultimately told him. He responded by confirming her account—and then some. "If I'm completely honest with you I can't see there being anything romantic between you and me because I see you as a little sister in here now," he said. Not only was Sharon friend-zoned—she was *sister*-zoned.

If you've ever been friend-zoned, you know what it feels like: shitty. Especially if it happens to you over and over again, you wonder if there's something about the energy you're putting out into the world that reads to the people you like as "I AM NOT A SEXUAL BEING!" You wonder whether it means you're bad at flirting, or you're not good/funny/smart/hot/insert-whatever-you're-most-insecure-about enough. It doesn't mean any of those things. All it means is that the other person just straight-up isn't interested in anything more than friendship, and as much as that sucks to hear, you've got to respect their honesty and move on. There are, after all, a lot worse ways to turn somebody down.

But if you've ever been in the other position—the one who has to do the friend-zoning—you know that it can often be even more difficult. If you're a woman who dates men, you know you're dealing with a group of people who are notoriously sensitive to the concept of friend-zoning, who see it as a case of women being "teases" or "leading them on" or a blight on the entire sex that women are "never into nice guys." (If someone you've rejected complains about girls not picking the "nice guy," first of all, that guy is not nice. Second, just because a few women rejected you doesn't mean all women are evil. Believing that stuff is how dudes end up falling for angry misogynist incel garbage to the point where they're guaranteed never to go on another date in their life.) A lot of times, that fear that men will react poorly (or violently) can lead women to delay the inevitable friend-zone conversation, the one where you put your cards on the table and say you'd like to keep the relationship platonic. But almost always in these cases, it's best to rip the Band-Aid off quickly, kindly, and firmly. Once he makes his feelings clear, or tries to make a move on you, tell him you appreciate him as a person but aren't interested in anything more than friendship. Remind yourself that you have nothing to feel guilty about, and a friend worth keeping will understand that. If he doesn't, or if he gives you some bullshit about being a tease or whatever, it's likely that he never saw you as a friend to begin with. As much as that sucks, count yourself lucky to be a little lighter from dead weight like that.

But honestly, I sometimes think the friend zone doesn't—or rather, shouldn't—exist. At the very least, it's not always the most useful term to describe the many shades of gray that exist in relationships. You can have a friend who you maybe flirt with on rare occasions but still consider a buddy, even though a small part of you might wonder if you'd ever get together in the future. The truth is, you may never know for sure what your feelings are until the other person makes a move or you have a drunken make out on a night out. Friendships aren't fixed (why else would so many of our favorite romance tropes be "friends to lovers"?), and that's kind of the beautiful thing about them. Not all our relationships can be categorized as "friend" or "lover," and even the ones that are clearly designated can sometimes switch. Let yourself be open to it without the change destabilizing your entire sense of self.

Because friendships can often change, that's just another reason to never fall into the trap of "no new friends." It can be tempting to keep your close pals close and never expand beyond your besties, but believe me when I say that things can and will change. And that's a good thing!

One of the best ways to expand your social group is by introducing different groups of friends, thereby building an ever-widening network where everyone's mutual friends become friends with each other. I know people are often hesitant to do this—maybe they worry their friends will get along too well and they'll end up being left out, or that their friends won't vibe at all to the point where it creates a rift. To me, however, both of these outcomes are worth the benefits of having a stronger social safety net. (And if you really can't see past your own cost-benefit analysis here, remind yourself that the bigger your network, the more chances you have to get set up with one of *their* hot single friends.)

To that end, my other favorite way to strengthen and expand my social life is in forming clubs. These emphatically do not need to be the normal kind of clubs, like book clubs, running clubs, or knitting clubs (although all three are fun!). These can be "hey, let's have a standing time every week to co-work on the creative projects we're both doing in our spare time" clubs, or grocery clubs, where you all shop for groceries together. Hell, why not start a *Love Island* club for nightly viewings every summer? A few years ago a couple friends and I would meet monthly to discuss how well our New Year's resolutions were going (like most New Year's resolutions, it fizzled after a few months). But the point here is less about the activity you're doing and more about having a set time and place on a regular schedule where you see the same people. I find it to be a much easier and low-pressure way to get to know new friends than randomly reaching out to grab dinner or drinks every once in a while, with the added benefit of hanging out with multiple folks at once. (And who knows, maybe one of those people could turn into something more than friends?)

In Lane Moore's book *You Will Find Your People: How to Make Meaningful Friendships as an Adult*, she lists a series of even more ways to expand and strengthen your social network. These steps can start from the couch: First, she recommends messaging someone you often interact with online—say, that one girl who likes all your Instagram Stories, the mutual acquaintance you only know from the internet, or the coworker you only interact with via Teams or Slack—and striking up a one-on-one chat in the DMs. Over time, those can translate into IRL meetups, or at the very least more frequent conversations.

Moore also suggests dipping your toe into the enormous network of your existing friends' other friends, and that includes their significant others. Inviting them to a party or a solo hang shows you think they're cool, and chances are they'll receive it as the compliment you intended it to be. Attending events—like concerts, comedy shows, fitness classes, or even restaurants and dog parks—alone can increase your chances of meeting someone new. Most of all, she recommends honoring the plans you've made with your friends, even when you'd rather sit at home alone on your couch.

Because the older you get, the more you'll be able to see that good relationships—especially platonic ones—are one of the biggest contributors, if not *the* biggest, to your overall happiness and quality of life. "As a woman in my thirties, my girlies have been the most important relationships, full stop. These are relationships that have taught me giddiness, fun, patience, spontaneity, loss, forgiveness. I've never had more friends, and I feel so blessed by that," says Liza.

"These relationships show us how to love and be loved and how to care for one another," adds Charlotte. "They soften us and can teach us how to be vulnerable, things that are valuable to understand when entering into a romantic relationship."

Lindsey, meanwhile, points out how bizarre it is that we expect our romantic partner to fill all of our time and fulfill all of our needs. "The amount of people in my life who seem to be worried or sad for me that I don't have a romantic partner is astounding," she says. "It makes me sad for them that they can't seem to understand that I have a very full and wonderful life on my own, with my friends! You can't get everything from one person."

"My platonic friendships are my soulmates," says Lydia. "It's harder with age because most of my friends are married, but eventually some will see the light and be divorced and orbit back to me. My platonic friends show up for me in ways no partner ever has, with no strings attached. Truly unconditional love. It's beautiful!"

Of all people, Aaron should have understood how wrong he was to say that "it's not fucking 'Friendship Island'": After his time on the show, *The New York Times* interviewed him and his castmate Rob about their hilarious but often lowkey moving bromance, which was edited into TikTok fancams and was one of the most delightful aspects of his season.

Thankfully, he took back his original statement. "I do agree it is also 'Friendship Island,' it's not just *Love Island*," he admitted to the paper. "Looking back on it now, obviously it's the relationships that you build on the way." It's probably the wisest thing he's ever said.

Key Takeaways:

- Dating without the support of solid friendships is a miserable experience. Platonic friendships are often the number one source of meaning and happiness in a person's life—your friends will show up for you in a way that the people you're dating can't.

- Someone might have feelings for you, and you just don't see them that way. In those cases, it's best to have the friend-zone conversation quickly, kindly, and firmly. A good buddy will understand and respect your honesty.

- If you sense a friendship moving into something more serious, be open to it! (Why else would "friends to lovers" be such a popular rom-com category?!)

- Resist the urge to have "no new friends." Friendships evolve, friend groups dissipate, especially as you get older. Always be open to making new connections and expanding your social network. Introduce people to each other, play host, form clubs, and reach out to internet pals to hang IRL.

Twelve

PIED OFF

It's extremely satisfying to watch the women of the *Love Island* villa call out bad behavior from the boys, especially considering how often they seem to get away with it. Neither the islanders nor the public is immune to the tired old refrain "boys will be boys," after all, which means that when the script is flipped, it's beautifully cathartic.

I can't remember a time of feeling such catharsis as in season 7, after Millie finds out that her partner Liam had been hooking up in Casa Amor with a woman named—I wish I were making this up—Lillie. Not only had she not known about it, given the producers hadn't revealed any foul play and Liam had returned to the main villa single and ready to couple up with her again, but he also lied to her about how many times they kissed and downplayed his connection with Lillie. It was Lillie, ultimately, who had the horrible task of revealing to Millie just how deep it went.

Viewers cheered when Millie took her at her word and confronted Liam about his lies. "I personally don't think I can go forward with this, because you've hurt me and I don't trust you," she tells him after he tries to make excuses. Then she gets up and walks away, much to the gratification of women everywhere.

But over the next few episodes, Liam tries to win her back. And somehow, it works: Soon afterward, Liam and Millie are coupled up again and seemingly happy. They'd go on to win the show.

While many fans worried about the message Millie taking back Liam sent to viewers at home—that a man can do whatever he wants and get away with it as long as he's nice to you after—I actually think Millie's reaction was a great representation of someone who stood up to someone who lied to them, called them out on it without apology, *and* was also open to seeing whether or not they're willing to change.

A lot of us, especially women, fear that if we ever express our true feelings, it's game over. We force ourselves to stay quiet and tamp down our anger because we worry it'll drive the people we love away. Millie, meanwhile, showed that you can get mad, you can be clear and strong and righteous in your fury, and the person on the receiving end won't necessarily be scared off. In fact, often the opposite happens: The person you're dating will respect the fact that you stood up for yourself, that you know your worth, and that you're protective about who you spend your time with. They'll see you for the prize that you are and work even harder to earn your trust back by correcting their behavior.

"They always come back," my friend Lindsey loves to say, referring to the dozens of times she's broken things off with a guy, just to see them orbit around in a few months or even years. She's right: You can tell a guy off, list everything he's ever done to piss you off, demand he do better, and if he wants to, sometimes he just . . . will? (If he doesn't, he probably just didn't want to, and you have no business being with a guy who doesn't want to—see chapter 17.)

If you're conflict-avoidant like me, this can be a pretty mindset-altering reminder that your world won't collapse if you stand up for yourself. People-pleasers tend to struggle with this: the idea that demanding an inch of space when it feels like you've been subconsciously shrinking yourself can actually *improve* a relationship.

It happened to my friend Kat in the early stages of dating her partner. "He came on super strong at first, and I told him I couldn't promise him anything," she says. That was until he got drunk one night and began texting her, professing his love and coming on even stronger than he had before. "I was like, 'Dude! I *just* said I wasn't ready for that, and that I needed some space.'"

Then, a curious thing happened. He gave her space. "We met for dinner and he was super receptive to why I had felt the way I felt, and genuinely apologized," she says. "I think it might have been the first time someone I was dating had actually taken accountability, so it was a no-brainer to forgive him. He moved much slower after that, and the rest is history!"

Conflict, ultimately, is a normal part of healthy relationships. When it happens for the first time, it can feel extremely destabilizing, like the person you thought you knew is someone else entirely. But it's worth remembering that it's actually a good sign, a sign that the argument is worth having in the hopes that it'll lead to a better dynamic down the line. Conflict is unavoidable in any relationship, and it can show you tons about how the other person operates, and in turn, they'll get to know you better, too.

One study of more than sixty couples found that more direct communication strategies, whether they were positive or negative, worked better to address the couples' problems long term—even if they caused discomfort in the moment. The lead researcher told *The Washington Post* that tough emotions like anger and hostility are useful both because they convey investment in the relationship and also make clear to both parties that this is a problem both people need to help to resolve. Other research shows that "couples who argue effectively are ten times more likely to have a happy relationship than those who sweep difficult issues under the carpet," according to one survey.

Or maybe you're one of those beautiful people who isn't conflict-avoidant. (First of all: How are you like this? Please teach me your ways!) It's possible you have the complete opposite problem, and that you feel as though no one will ever live up to your expectations, that you're constantly disappointed in the people you're dating and no amount of yelling or complaining or nagging will get them to change.

If this is you, trust me, I get it. In dating, people will never fail to disappoint you, and they'll do so in the most creative ways imaginable. But this, I think, is where picking your battles comes in handy. One good way of thinking about which battles are worth the fight is figuring out whether the problem is an ick or a dealbreaker. Remember the difference between surface-level complaints and serious red flags? These are good things to ask yourself: Is the thing you're annoyed by a little bit superficial? Or, if it doesn't change, could you see yourself ending the relationship?

That's not to say that you need to completely swallow every issue you have with a partner that isn't a total dealbreaker. It's just that there are kind ways to do this, and not-so-kind ways. The more significant the issue is, the more resolute you should be in your delivery, and the less willing you need to be to accept a compromise.

Let's say the person you're dating has been super flaky lately. They're constantly canceling plans at the last minute, and even though they apologize profusely and their excuses seem legit, you're starting to get really annoyed. If it had only been once or twice, sure, whatever, life happens. But consistently? Time to say something. The next time you see them IRL, bring it up by saying, "Listen, I get that work's been stressful, but when you're always moving our plans around or canceling it makes me feel like you don't value my time at all." If they assure you that it's only a temporary thing (maybe they've got a big project coming up) or if they truly seem to understand how shitty it feels and sincerely apologize, there's a good chance they're generally receptive to it when you bring up issues in the relationship. If they're defensive (or if they think you're being too demanding or clingy), they're either trying to shut you down without really understanding your perspective, or they're sensitive to conflict to the point where they can barely have even the simplest of difficult conversations. Not a great sign.

At the same time, it's almost always possible to compromise—this is the backbone of any relationship, and not just romantic ones. Compromising is great not just because it allows both parties to "win," but it also prevents any one party from feeling like the victim and the other from feeling like the perpetrator, thereby setting up a dynamic that can infect any later conflicts.

Then there are the arguments that often can't be resolved just by talking about it and standing up for yourself. I am, of course, referring to cheating, a topic so inflammatory and controversial that we could devote an entire book to talking only about that (and many authors have). Because we don't have an entire book's worth of time here and every infidelity is packed with its own infinite situational nuances, however, I'll focus on a problem that's much more relevant when you're just starting to date someone, which is: When is it okay to be angry or hurt that the person you're dating is also seeing other people, and vice versa?

This can be super tricky if you haven't had the exclusivity talk yet. Maybe you've been talking or casually dating for months, and you're extremely interested in a relationship, but you're too nervous to ask them to make it official. Then you find out the person is dating other people, too. It's an awful feeling, and you have every right to feel hurt and annoyed.

The problem is, though, that doesn't mean you have the right to be possessive or territorial about how the other person is spending their time. We live in the twenty-first century, not the nineteenth. The freedom to casually date multiple people at once was hard-won, even though it can sometimes make things complicated. If you're feeling hurt by this, that's a sign that you're interested in taking things to the next level, and it means it's time to have the define-the-relationship talk, however scary that might be.

Instead of attacking the person for dating other people or being passive-aggressive about how your feelings are hurt, keep the conversation about the two of you, and don't ask invasive questions about the other people they're seeing. Instead, start by saying something like "I know we haven't discussed this yet, but I'm wondering what you think about the idea of being exclusive, or whether you see us heading in that direction." Before you do so, be prepared for them to potentially tell you they're not ready for that just yet. Everyone dates on their own timeline, and not everyone is ready to jump into a relationship at the same exact moment. That's okay! It doesn't mean you should wait around for them forever—and it also doesn't mean you must cut them off immediately.

What's more important, regardless of their answer, is how they engage in that type of conversation with you. Are they panicky, avoidant, or defensive? That might mean they're not great at discussing more serious matters in general, a quality that makes a communicative relationship pretty damn difficult. Are they willing to hear you out, receptive to your feelings, and open to discussing the terms of the relationship? Great! That's a solid place to start, even if you don't end up making things exclusive just yet. They might be someone for whom it's worth waiting a little while. (At the same time, it's perfectly reasonable for you to decide that if they're still not ready in, say, three more months or whatever timeline you're comfortable with, then it's time to move on.)

Same goes for if someone you're dating starts acting a little territorial over who else you're seeing. You're well within your rights to date more than one person at a time if you haven't had the exclusivity talk yet. If someone's being demanding or judgmental about that, that could be a sign of future possessiveness (or worse, controlling behavior), and is worth keeping an eye out for.

In dating scenarios, a combination of trusting your gut and talking things out with friends (or your handy journal) is usually the best call. If there's a voice inside your head telling you to end things, it's usually worth listening to, because chances are it's not the first time that voice has made itself heard, nor will it be the last. Then again, if you explain the situation to a friend and they bring up how you're constantly running away from promising relationships the moment things get a little tough, listen to them! This is why recognizing your own potentially destructive patterns is crucial!

When you're dating, you will often be peppered with advice from social media (and potentially your friends) telling you that "if he does X, he's trash" or "if he doesn't do X, dump him." Some of it is good advice. Some is just kind of bitchy and judgmental. Places like TikTok offer short, snappy advice that's often reductive, and more entertaining than helpful. Put your phone down, tune out the noise, and think about what YOU want. Finding that out is harder than you'd think, but it's no less valuable.

You are, at the same time, not obligated to forgive anyone who harms you. Feeling constantly let down by someone you're dating is not normal. If your first thought when you think about them is stress, anxiety, or dread, you probably shouldn't be in a relationship. You are allowed to ask for an apology, to bring up issues that bother you, and to let go of people who've run out of chances.

Dating is messy. People will disappoint you (every once in a while is normal!), they'll say they're going to text and then forget. They'll speak without thinking in front of people you're trying to impress, they'll disagree on things you think are common sense. They'll cancel at the last minute and hurt your feelings in ways you didn't think anyone could. It's enough to make anyone wonder why we put up with other people at all.

But it's important to remember that if we cut out every single person who ever hurt us even a little bit, we'd all be living in tiny, isolated pods a safe six feet from each other. And that's no way to live. Chances are, you've also hurt people as well, and understanding the art of a thoughtful apology is just as important as learning how to use your voice and stand up for yourself when it matters most.

I'm sure Millie, for her part, is glad she forgave Liam after his Casa Amor debacle. Four years later, they're still together, laughing about their time on the show on their joint podcast. But I bet she's just as glad she called him out back then, too.

Key Takeaways:

- Bringing up issues in a relationship can actually make it stronger. Don't be afraid of conflict—it's a natural and healthy part of dating.
- Pay attention to how the person handles difficult discussions. If they're defensive and avoidant, it won't make for a healthy, communicative relationship. If they're willing to hear and understand your concerns while clearly laying out their own feelings, that's a great place to start.
- Not every issue needs to be a dealbreaker.
- It's okay to feel surprised and hurt if someone you're casually dating is also dating someone else. But until you're exclusive, it's on you to communicate your needs.
- People will disappoint you. Pick your battles wisely.
- The right person won't end things just because you expressed your desires or boundaries.

Thirteen

TWO BIRDS, ONE VILLA

Queerness, for obvious logistical reasons, throws a bit of a wrench into the mechanics of *Love Island*. It's a show where the constant musical chairs of "coupling up" necessitates a highly orchestrated revolving door in which the number of men and women are optimally matched to create the maximum amount of drama. For the most part, it works, if by "works," we mean people regularly get dumped and leave in tears. But what happens when the islanders' emotions don't align with the producers' aims?

It ultimately only took one and a half seasons for *Love Island* to figure out what that might look like. Toward the end of season 2, Katie entered the villa and immediately had her eye on Sophie. Though they shared a great date together and coupled up afterward, their relationship didn't last long—Sophie elected to leave the villa just two days later because she couldn't shake her feelings for Tom, who'd previously been dumped. A similarly brief romance blossomed in *Love Island* US season 5, when Kassy and Johnnie, having both decided to end things with the same man, realized they had feelings for each other, though they never became an official pairing. That's not to mention the several islanders who came out either before, during, or after their time on the show, including season 5's Curtis and Amber, season 7's Sharon, and *Love Island* US's Kyra, Courtney, and Nicholas.

That's a pretty decent number of bisexuals for what otherwise might be considered the straightest reality TV show ever (just kidding—that's obviously *The Bachelor*). Many of them have since spoken out about how they wish there was more representation of queerness on the show—a great point, considering it's treated as a "wrench" that audiences find compelling.

It's easy to feel that by coming out you're throwing a similar wrench into a life that otherwise would have looked a certain way or followed an expected path. Maybe you're worried about disturbing the version of you that exists in your head, or your family's heads, or your friends' heads. But guess what? You're not stuck in a villa where there are arbitrary rules about how many women and men can compete for love. You're not forced to couple up with someone even if you don't like them. You're in the real world, living *your* life.

And maybe that life could end up a little more colorful than you anticipated.

Something funny happened to me and many of my girlfriends during the pandemic. That thing we'd always wondered about ourselves, the thing inside of us that questioned whether we were only attracted to men, whether we'd previously acted on it or not, became too big and loud to ignore. We all have different reasons for this; for some of us, our social media algorithms knew before we did. Suddenly, our entire feeds were filled with queer people living their lives and being hot and we thought, "Wait, *I* want that." Some of us had spent so much time alone and inside with our own thoughts that the lack of external distractions made us more able to listen to what our inner selves were trying to tell us. That same isolation gave others the space they needed to be the person they wanted to be, without judgment. In most cases, it was a confirmation of something we'd long suspected rather than a surprise earth-shattering strike of lightning (though if a natural disaster comes down from the heavens and tells you you're gay, maybe you should listen!). Perhaps it took a global health crisis to get us to realize that life is short, and you might as well kiss who you want to be kissing.

Anyway, in the span of about a year, about half of my entire friend group was made up of bisexual women who'd mostly dated men. (This makes us very popular within the queer community. Lol—we'll get to that later.) For some of us, that meant finding ways to embrace our sexuality even if we were in hetero relationships, while for others it meant going out into the world and dating women as a woman for the first time. And that can be really terrifying.

"It's fucking hard. It's like being a virgin again who knows nothing," as Caroline puts it. Or, as Laura commiserates, "I'm kind of flopping at it. The hardest part is rewiring the flirtation game and figuring out the line between friendship and if you're going to date."

It worked out differently for all of us, but for the sake of a great story, I'll tell you about Sara. If you've ever felt like a late bloomer, or worried that you're coming to a realization about your sexuality at an older age than you think you're supposed to, there's a good chance you'll relate. (Which is great for you, because Sara is the best.)

"There was always some part of me that knew," she tells me over margaritas. "I'd always feel uncomfortable in the locker room and try to be respectful of people's privacy—everyone would joke that I was the prude."

It didn't help that Sara was also raised extremely religious and enrolled in programs that taught young girls that their only value was in their "purity"—meaning that your one goal in life is to be a virgin until you get married, and then presumably have lots of babies. These programs also, as they so often do, impart that homosexuality is a sin—something many people raised in religious traditions struggle with unlearning as they get older.

In college, Sara embodied the typical Southern sorority girl, but, she says, she'd often get drunk, black out, and then end up crying in bathrooms over a feeling she couldn't quite name. "I have this memory of being like, 'I think I'm gay,' and then crying about it, and I pushed it so far down that literally within the past year is when I remembered it," she says. "I was like, 'No, I can't be. I'm a sorority girl in Alabama!'"

Instead, she channeled her anxieties into a prodigious "hoe phase" (who among us hasn't had one?), though she often would ask herself why she never seemed to enjoy it as much as other people did. "At some point I was like, 'Why am I always blackout when I'm having sex with men?' And then at some point it kind of clicked."

It wasn't until her midtwenties that she, for the first time, said out loud to herself, "I am bisexual." "The second it happened, I was like, 'That was a profound moment,'" she says. "It was a turning point, where I'm admitting that I know this about myself, instead of just knowing and pretending it's not a thing."

After that, she started by adding women to her dating app pool—a small but crucial change that's often the first step toward coming into one's own queerness. A reminder at this particular stage: Even if you don't make a solid connection on date one doesn't mean you're not queer, just like going on a date with a man you don't connect with doesn't make you not interested in men.

As much as things felt like they finally clicked into place, it wasn't as though everything was smooth sailing from the get-go. For many people, young or old, their first sense of what queerness looks like comes from social media, meaning that the first thing many baby queers (that is, newly out queer people) hear is that nobody will like them or take them seriously. That in turn leads them to feel like they're not gay enough to exist in LGBTQ spaces, but too gay for straight societal expectations. Like many of us, Sara's social media feeds had begun serving her tons of queer content even before she came out. But instead of feeling like a warm welcome or a beckoning call into the community, it sometimes seemed like a giant KEEP OUT sign. On TikTok, she'd see content that delegitimized bisexuals as just straight people looking for attention or as girls who wanted the social clout of calling themselves queer without the risk and stigma that comes with it, or warning that bi women only use other women for sex and will ultimately ditch them for a man.

Here's the thing about some of that stuff: While I understand that it feels cathartic and protective to draw a clear line about who gets to belong in what community and who doesn't, and that it's extremely frustrating to feel like your identity is something that other people get to just try on, experiment with, and then toss away when it's no longer desirable for them, none of it justifies biphobia or painting all bisexual people with the same brush (our pride flag famously has three colors, after all). Queerness is not a limited resource. There are infinite ways to be queer, even if it doesn't look like what you see online.

Because in actuality, there are a fuck ton of bisexuals: 11 percent of eighteen- to twenty-nine-year-old Americans are bi, and bi people make up 60 percent of all queer folks in the US. That's most of them! Sixteen percent of American women under thirty are bisexual, but we're also far less likely to be out to those closest to us. While 75 percent of gay and lesbian people are out to the important people in their lives, only 19 percent of bisexuals are.

There are a million reasons why people don't come out: They aren't in a safe place to do so, they fear they'll be kicked out of their homes, fired from their jobs, or ostracized by the people closest to them. They fear violence, hate, and ignorance. For bisexual people, homophobia is only one side of the equation. It can feel unnecessary to alert your friends or family about your queerness if you've exclusively dated the opposite sex, but a big part of it is also due to the stigma from within and outside of the queer community toward bisexuality. It can feel like you're straddling two worlds, neither of which truly get it, or you.

Comphet, or the idea that society's default expectation for every-one is that they are heterosexual, can also be especially tricky to unlearn as a woman when kissing girls or otherwise showing phys-ical affection is seen as playful and unserious (in part because it appeals to men). Suddenly you start to wonder whether past crushes on men really were crushes after all, or if it was just compulsory het-erosexuality. It can make you doubt yourself and your desires, but noticing the ways it has affected your life and your choices is the first step to moving past it.

Katie Salmon from *Love Island* season 2 talked about experienc-ing hostility from both LGBTQ and straight people after her time on the show, and that she was fetishized by straight men and criticized from the queer community, who "treated it like it was nothing." Sara also dealt with this in her queer friendships, where she often felt like she wasn't queer enough to belong. They'd ask whether she'd ever hooked up with a girl before in a way that implied she wasn't "really" gay, or were judgmental when other people didn't fit the mold of what queer women are "supposed" to look like. "If queer people are making you feel bad about your level of queerness, they're not your friends," she says. "Find a different group."

Mean girl behavior is obviously nothing new, but when it hinges on a certain identity, it feels even worse, like that you've failed not only in being cool enough for people to want to hang out with, but that you've failed at something that's supposed to be intrinsic about your personhood. It's like middle school all over again, except this time with more nose piercings.

Then there's the part of queer friendships that gets even more complicated than the typical cliquishness. By this, I mean the inevi-table scenario where someone catches feelings or hooks up. I'm here to tell you: This happens *literally all the time*, so you might as well get used to it now.

That can sound scary if you've been in straight friend groups where two people hooking up caused a huge rift, or a big breakup made it so that you couldn't hang out all together again without it being super weird. But in queer friend groups, I've since learned that it's kind of the exact opposite. I'm not saying feelings don't get hurt or it never gets messy (dear God, does it get messy). It's just that people tend to be a lot more chill about hookups between friends because of how common it is. You have a night out with your girls, and suddenly you're making out on the dance floor and you spend the night at the other's place. Does that mean you're in love with them? Maybe! But it could just as easily mean that you're both attracted to each other in the moment and want to feel free to act on your feelings, even though you both acknowledge that you're not suddenly bound to the typical hetero courtship script where the next day someone has to text the other to see if they want to get a drink. Of course, you could still do that if you want! It just doesn't *have* to look like that.

If you do find yourself having strong feelings toward a friend, it's best to find out if they're interested in women before things move forward. "My advice is: Don't date straight girls or girls who act like they're straight," says Sara. "A lot of times, those girls have a lot of internalized homophobia and they're struggling with their own dismantling of expectations."

I've seen friends fall for someone, only to have the person hook up with them behind closed doors, then pretend like it never happened in a way that ended up being extremely dehumanizing for the other person. If this does happen to you, first of all: Their discomfort in themselves has absolutely nothing to do with you. Take a break from being around them, but not before letting them know how you feel, how you were hurt, and that you hope they can respect your space for the time being. Second, blast Chappell Roan's "Good Luck, Babe!" and scream-sing to it at karaoke to fully unleash the rage. Getting rejected by a female friend can sometimes feel doubly worse than getting rejected by a random dude you're dating—your friends, after all, are supposed to be the people who pick you up when your romantic life feels like it's spiraling down the drain, not the causes of it!

The real cure for this, however, is to find women to flirt with who aren't already your friends. Newly out bisexual women are often absolutely *terrified* of this: They think learning to flirt with women is as difficult as learning a second language. To be fair, it is different from flirting with men, but that's because I'd argue that it's secretly much easier. The good and the bad thing about being a woman who dates women is that pretty much everyone is constantly so afraid of approaching each other that if you decide that you're going to be the asker-outer, everything becomes pretty simple.

This works best when you're crystal clear and to the point: The next time you find yourself talking to a girl you think is cute, you can literally just be like, "You're super cute, are you straight?" If she is straight, she'll take that compliment and cherish it for the rest of her life, and you can move along. If she's not, keep chatting and ask her if she wants to grab a drink or a coffee this week. (If she is somehow offended by this question, she's homophobic and that sucks for her!) And if you feel like there's a vibe in the air and you're in that sexy little limbo period where you're unsure if you're about to kiss, it's a lot less weird to ask for consent than with a dude. A simple "Can I kiss you?" can be really hot in the right context.

Sara also recommends visiting your local queer bar and striking up conversations wherever you can, specifically by reaching out to people who might be there alone. Just like you, they're putting themselves out there to meet new people, and you can make it easier on both of you by approaching them first. Of course it's a little scary, but you can start small by turning your body toward the crowd and scanning the room to see who's receptive to eye contact. "One time I noticed a girl at a bar who was really beautiful and looked so confident, and I could tell she was there alone. I was like, 'That's badass that she came to this bar by herself.'" So she went up and asked if she'd like to join her group. They ended up making out and having a fabulous time. "The thing is: Be a girl's girl. Be a friend. And then if there's a vibe, great!"

This can be difficult for people in small towns without a thriving diverse queer community. "In smaller towns, it's about putting yourself out there, like joining a queer sports league, or going to the one queer bar in your area for trivia night," says Sara. "You've got to be really uncomfortable if you want to meet new people. It's going to be awkward the first few times you hang out, but keep going."

The internet and dating apps can also be a crucial lifeline if you're in a rural area. The key with dating apps, though, is to not fall into that common trap that a lot of women do with each other. I'll play it out for you:

WOMAN 1 [MATCHES WITH WOMAN 2]: you're sooooo pretty!
WOMAN 2: omg thank you so much! you're gorgeous as well!
WOMAN 1: ahhh thank you! ❤ ❤ ❤
WOMAN 1: [never says anything else ever again]
WOMAN 2: [does the same]

No! Bad! This is wrong! It is, unfortunately, quite common, though. "There are so many probably amazing women in my app graveyard, where we just never got past the 'Hi, hello' phase," says Sara. "If you're just, like, swiping and matching for the endorphins of it, you might actually be missing really good people in there. So being more intentional about the good people you match with is a good idea. There's a lot of people that I was just waiting for them to make the move, and now they're in the graveyard."

Luckily, there is a very easy solution to this, and it is called ASK HER OUT! Yes, you, newly out bisexual woman who potentially has never asked anyone out in her life! I know it sucks when it seems like no one's brave enough to make the first move, but guess what? You will be the change you wish to see in the world! Ask that girl out!

Trust me, she'll be thrilled. And if she isn't, that's one step closer to finding someone who is.

Or maybe you're just not there yet, and that's okay, too. We're told that the only way to be queer is to be loud and proud about it, but if you're still in the closet or for whatever reason not interested in making it a part of your public-facing self, there are still plenty of ways for you to honor that part of you. Because you *should* honor it! You can do so by enjoying and supporting queer art—books, music, films, TV shows (there are so many of them now!)—or creating some of your own. You can attend queer events, make queer friends, donate to queer causes, and speak out on behalf of queer rights. You can support queer-owned businesses in your area and read about the fascinating, inspiring, and sometimes devastating history of queer liberation.

And when and if you're ready to come out, there's a whole world waiting for you.

Like a lot of people, I was very resistant to putting a label on my sexuality at first. In my mind *everyone* was a little bisexual, so why bother making that a central part of my identity? And it wasn't like I was attracted to every single woman I've ever met, so how could I truly be bi? Looking back, this is a hilariously misguided way of determining one's sexuality; it's not like I was attracted to every guy I'd ever seen either (like, have you *met* men?). It's clear to me now that a lot of that is internalized biphobia and a way to be like, "Well, I'm not like *those* bisexuals, the ones who are evil and slutty and also probably faking it."

Anyway, cheers to being evil and slutty. It's more fun this way.

"I'm just so much happier now," Sara says. "I'm not crying in my dorm bathroom. I'm not crying in my bathroom at all, usually. So that's nice." It might have taken longer than you thought, but you're here now. And if you're still questioning your sexuality and feeling unsure about labels, remind yourself that you don't get a prize for figuring out your exact identity the fastest. In fact, there's a good chance your sexuality will evolve over time—you might use one label like fluid or bi or pan one year, and then realize you vibe more with another one the next. Though she originally came out as bisexual, Sara now refers to herself as a lesbian (or just "queer") but acknowledges that this might change.

As an out queer person, she often fields questions from women who identify as straight but are coming to the realization that they really like making out with girls, even if they couldn't imagine having sex with one. To those women, she says, "Maybe you might be bi! You don't have to put a label on it. If you think you might want to date women, go on some dates with women."

"The freedom is in the openness, in being like, 'I can flirt with that girl, I can flirt with that guy, I can flirt with that nonbinary person. None of it matters,'" says Sara. "We're on a floating rock. Kiss who you want to kiss!"

Sara eventually found the person she wanted to kiss on the floating rock—a woman who, ironically, was from her app graveyard. They both remember seeing each other on the site but never matched or messaged, and it wasn't until a mutual friend invited them both out that they realized they had incredible chemistry. "She was texting this other girl all night, and I don't know what came over me, but I was just drunk enough to be like, 'Are you gonna put your phone away and pay attention to me?'" They ended up making out that night, and the rest is herstory.

There is so much joy in the fluidity that bisexuality allows for. Even if I was wrong about my belief that everyone's a little bi (because every so often you meet someone who has literally never had a gay thought in their life, and you're like, "Oh wait, straight people *do* exist!"), I still feel like maybe the world would be more fun if people were less closed off to the possibility of it. And *Love Island* would be a better show if it embraced that, too.

Key Takeaways:

- If you want to date women, date women! Changing the settings on your dating app is a great place to start (and even if you don't click with the first girl you go out with, that doesn't mean you're not interested in women altogether).

- Don't date girls who behave like they're straight. They're probably working through some internalized homophobia and aren't quite ready for a relationship yet.

- Women who are just starting to date women are often scared to ask each other out. You can be the change you wish to see in the world! Ask her out, and don't let potential matches die in your app graveyard!

- If you're not ready to come out yet, there are tons of ways you can honor your queerness that don't involve dating or hooking up. When you are ready, there's a whole world waiting for you.

Fourteen

BEWARE OF DOGS (AND OTHER TYPES OF MEN)

Among the more quietly heartbreaking arcs in *Love Island* history is that of Amy and Curtis, the early season 5 power couple who fell for each other almost immediately. In the beginning, their chemistry was palpable, if a bit more wholesome and G-rated than the average *Love Island* pairing: Amy was quirky and more insecure than the legions of influencers and models who populate the island, in part due to the fact that she'd never been in a relationship before. Curtis, meanwhile, was the stereotypical Nice Guy, an effervescent dancer who acted as peacemaker and friend to all in the villa. When Amy felt uncomfortable, Curtis reassured her. On paper, he was doing everything right, and in the days leading up to Casa Amor, it seemed like Amy was on the verge of getting her first boyfriend.

Their relationship never quite got that far. By the time Casa Amor came around and he started to have feelings for another woman, Curtis had only ever referred to Amy as—humiliatingly—his "half girlfriend." When she returned to the villa, relieved to see he hadn't coupled up with anyone new, Amy was ready to put it all on the line—until, she soon found out, he was having "meaningful snogs" with another woman while she was away. Thus begins one of the most iconic line deliveries in villa history: "I was coming back here to tell you that I loved you," she snaps. Needless to say, he does not return the sentiment.

But there's another conversation that illustrates the mismatch in feelings between the two of them even more precisely. Later, Amy points out to him that she felt sad when all the other couples were cuddling in the morning and Curtis was always off somewhere else. "In the morning, if someone likes you, they want to have a cuddle in bed with you in the morning," she pleads. To this, he replies, "I know, and I also want to be the person who gets up and makes everyone a coffee so everyone's ready for the morning."

There are two ways to interpret this statement. One is that Curtis is a uniquely selfless individual, someone who puts the needs of others before his own. The other is that throughout their brief relationship, Curtis put Amy at the absolute bottom of the list of people he cared about making happy, and all of the other islanders at the top. The rest of the world was able to tell which one was truer than the other, and thankfully, so did Amy, who left the villa of her own accord soon after.

Curtis isn't a bad guy—before the Amy breakup, he was one of the more likable in the house, and he'd go on to place fourth overall by pairing up with Maura. Rather, he was a guy who valued being liked by the group more than being loved by the one person who ostensibly should matter most. Not only did he refuse to cuddle Amy in the mornings because he was busy making her coffee—he didn't do it because he was making everyone *else* coffee.

In internet parlance, Curtis was behaving like a golden retriever boyfriend. This is not necessarily an insult. In fact, finding a golden retriever boyfriend seems to be pretty high on many people's wish lists these days. "Fine, I Admit It—I, Too, Would Like a Golden Retriever Boyfriend," blares one *Cosmo* headline, which describes the type as "the human equivalent of a large, lovable house pet." *Elle* put together a list of "10 On-Screen Golden Retriever Boyfriends," including *Friends*' Chandler Bing and *The Office*'s Jim Halpert, both known best for being obsessed with their respective partners. According to the many, many memes and TikTok trends celebrating golden retriever boyfriends, they're known as unproblematic, emotionally available, and the total antithesis of the "bad boy." They've got BDE (Big Dad Energy) even when they don't have kids. They're actually nice to your friends, or at the very least, willingly engage in conversations with them—a rarity these days! They're kind, playful, and, maybe in some cases, are the littlest bit dim-witted, in a way that still manages to be endearing.

And I'm here to spoil the fun and argue that while golden retrievers might make great pets, they don't make good boyfriends.

Take, for instance, the two classic golden retriever boyfriends mentioned in the *Elle* listicle, Chandler Bing and Jim Halpert. Both ended up as loving and supportive spouses, for the most part, but consider how they treated their previous partners: Remember how shitty and cowardly Chandler was to Janice, whom he never actually seemed to like, or how Jim was just kind of faking it with Karen in an attempt to get over Pam? In both cases, they continued to go through the motions of relationships they didn't really want to be in, all because they were too scared to say how they really felt and risk disappointing the other person (and probably, of facing the prospect of being alone). It's precisely how Curtis treated Amy: like a placeholder, which, thank God, she eventually says to him outright.

Because golden retrievers *love* people. The problem is that it doesn't matter who, as long as said person is willing to scratch their neck and give them treats. They give and receive love without discernment, which is a great quality to have in a dog and a terrible quality to have in a partner who's supposed to be your teammate.

So why the obsession with golden retrievers, then? I'm convinced it has something to do with the ways men's relationship to masculinity has evolved throughout the course of the social media age. The internet connected more of us to each other, it opened the general public's eyes to all kinds of subcultures and aesthetics and modes of being a person. In so many ways, that's been beautiful, expanding our definitions of gender and its infinite expressions. In others, it's a brutal reminder of what happens when lonely, angry men connect online with the sole purpose of harassing everyone else who doesn't share their backward, patriarchal vision for the world. Because the internet helped put a name to certain categories of men, some of them are lauded as the perfect ideal, while others are walking red flags. The golden retriever boyfriend is the antithesis of the sad, lonely incel. They're too busy saying, "I'm good with whatever!" instead of just suggesting a time and place for a date. And I get it! One of those things is a lot more appealing than the other!

My friend Megan, for instance, specifically seeks out golden retrievers on the apps (her answer for the Hinge prompt "I'll fall for you if . . . " is "you've got big golden retriever energy but a sharp wit"). "I think of it as goofy and harmless," she explains. "It's, like, well-meaning—a himbo, but smart."

Her version of "golden retriever energy," though, isn't always what guys mean when they describe it themselves. "My ex was a self-described golden retriever and that motherfucker was so toxic," says Haley. "When I see a guy put 'golden retriever' in his bio it's an automatic nope from me," Lindsey adds. "It tells me that he's dumb and not serious or lazy."

"It's giving 'local idiot,'" Laura agrees. "The 'I'm just a goofy fun guy' schtick gets real old when you have to, like, plan a trip."

Golden retrievers aren't the only type that women should be on the lookout for when they're dating around. First and foremost is, of course, the Situationship Guy. In my day we called them fuckboys, otherwise known as the guy who can't (or more likely, won't) commit to one person at a time because they're constantly keeping their options open for someone better. They might be charming and fun to be around and perhaps even kind to your face, but the problem is that often they're only charming as a means to an end. Usually, that "end" is a loosely defined situationship with no mention of exclusivity (and don't even try to bring up the word "boyfriend" unless you want him to run away like a scared little puppy). The fuckboy *loves* a situationship. It allows him to behave entirely on his terms, because, well, there *are* no terms. The only applicable descriptor is a word with almost zero meaning—"situation"—which gives him pretty much free rein to do whatever he wants.

And yet the portmanteau "situationship" has somehow become an extremely popular means of describing a phenomenon so many women find themselves in. It doesn't have the charm and specificity of "friends with benefits," which, as I've already argued, can be wonderful, nor does it contain the dignity of "dating," because that scares him off. ("What's next, she'll start *expecting* things from me?") But if you're hanging out with someone somewhat regularly and also you're hooking up, guess what? That's dating. You can be dating multiple people, but to devalue something as special and exciting as the beginning stages of dating as a "situationship" is one of the many subtle ways we convince ourselves that we're not settling when we definitely are. If a guy you're seeing is too scared to use the term "dating," consider how much time and effort you're willing to devote to someone who can't even accurately describe what you're doing here.

Then there's the Finance Guy, which you can easily swap out with Entrepreneur Guy or Real Estate Guy or Tech Guy or Creative Director Guy or Artist Guy or basically any dude who uses his job as the primary marker of his identity. You might be wondering, "What does Artist Guy have remotely in common with Finance Guy?" Even though their clothes and their home and their friend group and their salary might be very different, their attitude is the same: They think they're better than you because of the title on their LinkedIn (or in the case of the Creative Director, their collection of vinyl records and annoying hats). Often, these types act like they're doing you a favor by being in your presence, while not having a single thing to contribute that doesn't revolve around themselves. They believe they can get away with treating you like shit because you should feel lucky to be there at all. Say it with me: Kindness is the bare minimum. They might seem impressive, or wealthy, or smart, or cool, but if they're not nice, it's on to the next.

This type also has a polar opposite, a guy who can be just as detrimental to your dating journey: the Loser. First of all, when did we as a society stop describing people as losers? I find it to be quite useful, actually, because what else are we supposed to call dudes who have no desires, no passion, no ability to take care of themselves, and expect you to be their mommy (and not in a fun kinky way, if you're into that)? I'm not referring to guys who don't make a ton of money or aren't attractive; I'm referring to guys who contribute nothing to society and still somehow have the gall to expect a superhot woman to float down from the heavens and fix their life for them. When you've been treated like an object by the Situationship Guy and spoken to like an idiot by the Finance Guy, the Loser can sometimes feel like a breath of fresh air—finally, here is someone who *appreciates* me!—but beware: The Loser, while expecting the world from you, is fundamentally incapable of understanding how to reciprocate. He can't even put in the effort to make his own life less shitty, never mind yours! He is a black hole, one that you could waste years of your life on sinking deeper and deeper into until it's impossible to climb out. You're not here to do a renovation on someone else's life, you're here to find someone you want to spend yours with. Don't waste it on a Loser.

Golden retrievers aren't even the only *dog*-related boyfriend stereotypes that exist online. Apparently there are now such things as Rottweiler boyfriends (wherein you hate everyone except your girlfriend), Doberman boyfriends (the strong and silent "protector"), German shepherd boyfriends (a slightly more affable version of the Doberman boyfriend), and borzoi boyfriends (quiet and aloof, the type of boyfriend to hide behind you at a party to avoid having to socialize). All of these, somehow, sound less pleasant than being with a golden retriever boyfriend, who, at the very least, is a good time.

You don't want a dog boyfriend. You want a boyfriend who, when you're at a party and you're a little tired and socialized-out, gives you a squeeze and offers to call the Uber. A golden retriever boyfriend will, sensing more fun to be had, beg you to stay just a little longer and then turn that into three more beers with the guys while you're trying not to fall asleep on the couch. You want a boyfriend who really engages with you when you're venting about your annoying coworker instead of telling you to just "be positive!" When you're coming out of a movie theater, you want a boyfriend who cares about your opinions and offers critical ones of his own, rather than just saying, "I liked it!"

You want a boyfriend who, when you ask why he won't cuddle you in the morning, asks for your favorite cuddling position. A golden retriever will be too busy making coffee for everyone else.

Key Takeaways:

- Proceed with caution if you're dating anyone who describes himself as (or acts like) a "golden retriever." Much like the dog, he wants everyone to love him and treats everyone like they're the most special person in the world. You want someone who makes *you* a priority.
- Proceed with caution if you're dating someone who's charming and fun but will run away like a scared little puppy if you even hint at the word "relationship."
- Proceed with caution if you're dating the type of guy who thinks they're a little bit better than you because of their job (whether it's in finance or if they're a self-described "creative director").
- Proceed with caution if you're dating . . . well, any man, really.

Fifteen

SAYING TA-TA TOGETHER

Toward the end of season 7, it seemed like the *Love Island* crown was Jake and Liberty's to lose. Since coupling up on day one, they'd been the most solid relationship in the villa, remaining loyal to each other even after a Casa Amor visit that proved disastrous for some of their fellow strongest couples.

So it shocked both audiences and their castmates when Jake and Liberty announced they were walking away from the chance to win it all, instead deciding to leave the villa as friends. It turned out that throughout their relationship, Liberty felt uncertain that Jake's feelings were genuine: She said "I love you" weeks before he returned the sentiment, and on movie night, she watched Jake admit he didn't want to "rip her clothes off." She worried she was giving him the ick because her sleeping area was a little messy, while some of the women expressed concern that he was playing a game. In an emotional conversation just days before the finale, she ultimately tells him that "I just don't feel like you love me for me, and I want someone who loves me for me."

What Liberty did takes a lot more strength than anyone realizes. It's *so* easy to settle for less than what you deserve, or even less than what you want. And most of the time, it's not like there's a big pot of money to win. People just get used to feeling a little dissatisfied. They resign themselves to a relationship that's a little lackluster, and being a little disappointed with the choices they've made. They do this because they're scared of change, they're scared of being alone, and they're scared of disappointing their partner, the other people in their lives, or their own expectations. Ironically, sometimes being a little uncomfortable can be the most comfortable thing in the world.

Her choice was especially commendable because she realized that even though she clearly genuinely loved Jake, he didn't feel the same and probably never would. That is a *really* hard thing to walk away from. You tell yourself they'll change, that someday they'll realize everything about you is actually wonderful, that they'll snap into suddenly behaving like the perfect partner.

But this is magical thinking, not reality. Which is why so often the stages of a dating scenario end up like this:

- It's happened! You've found someone to be with who wants to be with you! Everything is perfect and amazing and you think, oh my god, this is it!

- And then you wonder . . . is it?

- You begin to ask yourself, if this is, like, *it*-it, shouldn't I be happier? Or more excited to spend time with them? Or more satisfied?

- No, no, I'm overthinking. Everything's fine.

- Ugh, they're annoying me again. Why are they like this? Do they even like *me*?

- Wait, no, why am I being such a bitch? I should be grateful that someone wants to hang out with me all the time. Plus, they're really not that bad! I don't want to have to start over!

ENNGHHH!!! (This is my textual impression of a loud buzzer sound.) Stop it right there. Anytime you find yourself thinking some variation of the words "They're not really that bad" or "Do they even like me" or, the guiltiest culprit of all—"I don't want to have to start over"—it is a sign something is wrong.

Often this is the scariest thing about dating: the realization that the person you're with isn't the person you want to *keep* being with. It's terrifying enough that you'll delay the inevitable for as long as possible in the hopes that you're wrong or that they'll change. But just as they say in love—when you know, you know—the same is usually true for breaking up.

When I asked friends when they knew it was time to dump someone, their answers ranged from creative differences ("When I didn't care that he didn't come see my play") to sexual incompatibility ("When the thought of fucking him felt like a chore") to highly specific red flags ("When he had to do cocaine before dinner with my parents").

In most cases, what the breakup boiled down to was that one person clearly had stronger feelings than the other. Both of these positions—realizing that the other person likes you more than you like them, or being the person with the stronger feelings—are hard ones and can be equally painful, in different ways.

Amanda has been in both. In the first case, she says that the biggest sign that she needed to end things was when she didn't feel like she enjoyed her partner's company for an extended period of time anymore. She realized she lacked patience and felt edgy in his presence. At that point, she says, "it was kinder for me to end the relationship."

I've been there, too: There were times when, in previous relationships, I found myself overcome with anxiety, guilt, and resentment most of the times we were together, and let it go on for longer—in some cases years longer—than it ever should have. After we broke up and some time had passed, I went back and looked at the texts we used to send each other and was thrown off at how little emotion, or sometimes basic human kindness, was present in our interactions. It's shocking to me now, but at the time I was so used to the lack of romance that I ultimately settled for a relationship just comfortable enough to keep me unhappily inside of it. (If you're beginning to feel this way, try looking back on your text history with your partner and attempt to view it as objectively as you can. Do these sound like two people who like each other? Or do they sound like two annoyed roommates having a contest to see who can be the most passive-aggressive?)

Charlotte experienced something similar. "One telltale sign of if the relationship was doomed or not was whether or not I was judging the relationship on the memory or the potential of the person or the time I spent with the person themselves," she says. Her first serious relationship in college was with a guy she only saw on the weekends because he lived about an hour away. After a year, she found that while she really looked forward to her time with him when they were apart and enjoyed thinking back on their happiest memories, when the time came to spend the weekend with him, she was usually miserable the whole time. "My desire to pull the plug was at an all-time high when I was around him, and subdued as soon as he was gone. This was an obvious sign that it was time to move on," she recalls. "I could barely stand being around him by the end of it, and while I do still hold many fond memories of our earlier times together, it would've been insane to continue putting up with my weekly misery just for the romance of a memory."

The second scenario, though, is usually the harder one. Amanda says that one of the most painful parts is wanting to be around the other person even when you know it isn't a healthy relationship because they either clearly don't enjoy your company anymore or they explicitly tell you they're having doubts. "I think that's the point when you decide that you can't wait around any longer hoping that they'll change their behavior. That's when it's time to pull the plug," she says. "You have to remind yourself that you deserve someone who really delights in your company."

Otherwise, it's just another example of magical thinking, or believing something or someone will change and suddenly the relationship will be perfect again. "Great in theory" is meaningless. It's bullshit. The real question is: Do they make your life better *now*? Are they telling and showing and giving you what you need in a relationship, and are you giving it back to them? This can mean verbal affirmations, kept promises, thoughtful gestures, consistency, honest communication, or any of the other important qualities a good relationship needs. If the answer is no, it's time to have one of those really uncomfortable conversations and break out the brutal honesty.

Knowing when to end a relationship isn't a science (or even really an art). It's more about listening to your head, your heart, and your gut, and checking to see where they align. If your head and your gut both say it's time to leave, but your heart's still worried you'll hurt the other person, you could end up in a position where you're leading someone on for months on end, ultimately causing them even more pain. In that scenario, it would have been kinder to end it when you realized your head and your gut were both telling you this wasn't the right relationship for you.

I think we can all agree that breakups are best done kindly, empathetically, and privately. That means ideally in person, unless it's been under a month or so or if it's more of a casual on-and-off thing, in which case a thoughtful text can be appropriate. It means telling someone how you feel in a concise but openhearted way, without making excuses or assuming how they're going to respond. It means not overusing HR buzzwords or therapy jargon, e.g., "At this juncture I would like to set a boundary by terminating our contact while I continue on my self-care and healing journey" (I am so sorry you just had to read that sentence). And it also means sticking up for yourself and how you feel if they react poorly. No, it's not easy or fun, but you also don't owe anyone a relationship that's not working anymore.

If it's only been a few months, I think the same rules apply. A phone call, in that case, could be appropriate if you don't see each other often and live far from each other (who wants to go through the torture of an IRL breakup conversation followed by a forty-five-minute ride home?).

Friends-with-benefits situations, meanwhile, don't usually require you to make a huge deal about it. If you need to end things for whatever reason (maybe you met someone else you really like, or you sense they're catching feelings), the next time they ask you to meet up, just let them know you value their friendship but can't continue hooking up for the time being. If it was casual to begin with, they'll likely understand. Cut the tension by buying them a drink the next time you see them out as friends, and cheers to the fun times you had.

The rules for breaking up with someone you've only been out with once or twice, however, are completely different from the rules of dumping a partner. My personal favorite strategy for the former scenario may be a bit controversial, but here it is: I call it "mutual ghosting." I know what you're thinking: Ghosting is never okay under any circumstances! But mutual ghosting is a bit different.

Mutual ghosting is a practice that, if wielded properly, can do the impossible: end a relationship with both parties' dignities still intact. Like I said, it should only be used when you've only been out once or twice (or in other select circumstances, which I'll describe later). Here's how you do it:

Just don't text them, and hope they don't text you either. That's it!

You'd be surprised at how often people can feel when there's no real connection. So instead of sending that would-be obligatory "Hey, I really enjoyed our date, but I just wasn't feeling a romantic connection, good luck out there!" text that it feels like everyone sends these days, you just literally don't have to say anything.

If they ask you to go out again, that's when you are indeed obligated to send that go-to "let's end things" text. We're not doing the evil kind of ghosting here, the kind where you stop responding when the other person is trying to get a straight answer from you. But until they do, you're off the hook and free to pretend they never existed. Chances are, they'll do the same for you.

When I was dating, I never needed confirmation or an elaborate reason why a guy no longer wanted to date me. At that point, it wasn't my problem anymore, and I didn't really need the ego hit. And because of that, I'll never quite be convinced that all instances of ghosting are inherently evil. Sometimes we do it because we care—about each other, and about ourselves.

Ending a relationship, even a short one, is never easy. It's always an obstacle course of bruised egos and petty resentments and mismatched memories of what happened and who's to blame for it. But ultimately, every relationship ends in some amount of agreeing to disagree. In the case of Liberty and Jake, she realized that he didn't love her the way she wanted to be loved. He might disagree on the details, but what viewers can all agree on is that Liberty deserved better. And breaking up with Jake was the first step to getting it.

Key Takeaways:

- When determining whether it's time to break up with someone, listen to your head, your heart, and your gut, and check to see where they align. If two out of three agree, go with what they tell you.

- If you've only been on one or two dates with someone and you don't see it going any further, don't be too quick to send that standard "Hey, I'm not interested" text. Just don't text them at all—there's a good chance they didn't feel a spark either, and neither of you have to go through the ritual of rejecting each other. (It's called mutual ghosting!)

- Breakups for longer relationships should be done kindly, empathetically, and privately. You don't owe anyone a relationship, but you should still be treating each other like human beings.

Sixteen

SO YOU'VE BEEN DUMPED FROM THE
PROVERBIAL ISLAND

On *Love Island*, "getting dumped" has a double meaning. There's the usual way—your partner says they don't want to be with you anymore—and then there's the way that only applies if you're a contestant on the show, meaning that either the viewing public has decided they don't want to watch your search for love anymore, or that your fellow islanders have voted you out of the villa. (Honestly, hard to say which is worse?)

Oh, and not only that, but when you get dumped from *Love Island*, there's a good chance you're doing so while having to stand in a tiny bikini in front of all your friends and also millions of people at home.

Most of us probably will never know what it's like to have your lowest moment aired on a massively popular television show. But anyone who's ever had their heart broken knows the raw, intense vulnerability that comes with it, the feeling that even the slightest gust of wind could scatter you into pieces.

You could argue that the hardest part of dating is the consistent effort it takes—the time, money, and energy required to leave your house and sit across from a stranger, whom you often realize instantly isn't right for you, and then repeating this process over and over. You could argue that it's the disappointment after a date you were psyched for, one you told all your friends about, turns out to be less than magical. You could argue it's the creeping sense of dread that you'll never find something even remotely close to romantic love, that you've missed your chance, that something's seriously wrong with you because this thing that everyone else in your life seems to get so easily just hasn't happened yet for you.

But you'd be wrong. The hardest part of dating is the heartbreak that happens after someone you really care about tells you it's over.

Maybe they did it over text, maybe it was a long, tearful conversation. Maybe they didn't even give you the courtesy of telling you at all and they just straight-up ghosted. But ultimately, it doesn't matter how. The message is always the same: They don't want to date you anymore. And suddenly it becomes your job to figure out how to deal with that.

You might be surprised by the breakups that break you. It's not always the person you've been with the longest. It might not even be the other person who did the dumping. My worst breakup was one where I was technically the one initiating it. And do you know how many times I've cried over guys I was never even in a relationship with? Probably more times than I cried over a breakup with an ex I dated for years. The fact that a relationship that was meaningful to us never even had the dignity of a label can often make it worse: You never got to actually live out all those memories you imagined you'd make together, and you're grieving a potential that never materialized. On top of all that confusion and frustration over the lack of closure, your friends just don't get why you can't seem to get over a relationship that was never that serious, making you feel even more lonely and isolated than you already were.

In any case, after any relationship ends, no matter how serious or situational, we pore over what we supposedly did or said wrong, what's truly the matter with us, whether they could see something rotten inside of us that we couldn't. We romanticize our ex, we tell ourselves we missed our one chance at happiness, that we'll never find anyone as perfect, that this breakup is a sliding doors moment we'll always look back upon with regret: What kind of life could we have had if it had worked out, if we had been a little different?

No! Stop it. There is nothing wrong with you, and life is, if you're lucky, very long. Instead of spiraling, please refer to these ten 100 percent–guaranteed, surefire ways to completely get over someone. (Just kidding. The only one that really works is the last one, and you're gonna hate it.)

DO SOMETHING KIND OF INSANE WITH YOUR HAIR AND/OR PHYSICAL APPEARANCE

Hair grows back, after all. Listen, I'm not saying you should get a really heinous tattoo or wild haircut that screams to the world "I'M GOING THROUGH SOMETHING RIGHT NOW!" But I also think there's something kind of wholesome and almost romantic about leaning into post-breakup stereotypes that say you should go buck wild at the salon. A breakup can really rock your sense of self, and one way to assert who you are is to do so with beauty and fashion. When Charlotte was going through her bad breakup, she said she focused on developing her own identity. "I listened to music I loved, watched films, invested in hobbies I could do with my hands, bought clothes that made me feel confident, dyed my hair, and etched my skin," she says. I can confirm she's even cooler now because of it.

TRAVEL LIKE A MANIAC

A change of scenery can go a lot further than you think. Liza, ever the explorer, decided to work remotely from Austin, Texas, for a few months after her breakup, then took a road trip from Sedona to San Diego. "As Emma Roberts would say, 'intentional solitude!'" she says. "It ended at a wellness spa with the women in my family, [where we did] body work, meditations on happiness, art, writing, finding better for myself."

THROW YOURSELF INTO YOUR ART

Will it be bad art? Probably. But will it feel good to turn the mess of your mind into something tangible? Of course it will. Whenever I'm sad, I write really terrible poems in my Notes app while I'm on the subway. No one has ever read them, and God forbid anyone ever does, but I still try to make them sound as good as I possibly can for someone with hardly any poetry education, and they're quite precious to me.

THROW YOURSELF INTO THE GYM

I do not believe in the concept of a "revenge body," which is extremely depressing, but getting super into fitness isn't the worst way to deal with a breakup. The point is to *move* your body, not necessarily change it. Maybe that means getting out of bed and doing some stretches before you mindlessly open your phone and scroll for an hour, maybe that means hitting ten thousand steps a day, maybe it means getting really into weight lifting. Exercise is basically a free antidepressant with none of the side effects. Take advantage!

FEEL YOUR FEELINGS

The thing that used to scare me away from therapy was the idea that this was suddenly a thing I had to do *forever*. This is not the case! Therapy is great, even in small doses when you're engaging with it for a specific purpose, like grief or heartbreak. A therapist can give you the space to actually feel the things you're fighting against, if only for forty-five minutes every week. You'll learn grounding techniques and be able to talk through harmful beliefs you may have about yourself—the usual stuff we tell ourselves, like we're not enough, or that we're too much for anyone to truly love—and figure out where these beliefs stem from.

After Amanda got divorced, she gave herself the gift of actually grieving her marriage rather than just convincing herself to push through it before she was ready. "The only thing that got me through was allowing myself to grieve for quite a while," she says. Thanks to her flexible job, she moved in with her mom for six months after the split. "It's cliché, but sometimes the only way out is through. I think I just needed a long, slow emotional purge. I'm not saying I was magically healed in six months, but just letting myself be sad without immediately trying to 'get back out there' really, really helped."

Even the best of us get sucked into the fantasy that we can outsmart our feelings or intellectualize them into never having existed in the first place. But big feelings have a funny way of showing themselves if they're not recognized and honored. Let yourself miss your ex and feel the grief that comes with it. It's the only way to move on to the greener pastures of acceptance.

ENGAGE IN FUN, ALBEIT RISKY, BEHAVIORS

This is sort of exactly the opposite of the previous bit of advice, but sometimes when the world wants you to shut yourself away and heal in peace, the best thing you can do for yourself is allow your freak flag to fly a little bit. I'm not saying have sex with every person that comes across your Tinder feed, but I am saying that a dance floor make-out session is often more ego-boosting and life-affirming than even the best therapy session.

"I fucked my way through half the London comedy scene," recalls Sylvie of her breakup. Laura, meanwhile, got over a brutal three-year situationship by making out with random people in bars, then "diving back into dating with a new resolve and a new unwillingness to take shit." She met her next boyfriend three weeks later. Rebounds get a bad rap, but personally I've met several of my exes while rebounding from a different one. And on some level, aren't we all on the rebound from something?

GET OUT OF YOUR HEAD

Yes, your job right now is to focus on yourself, but don't "focus on yourself" to the point you're neglecting the people that make life worth living. "I made sure to always say yes when people texted me to do something," says Andrew of his worst breakup. This is key, as is becoming the kind of person who's regularly asking people to hang out or organizing events, especially if this doesn't come naturally to you.

One of the best pieces of advice I've ever received was that when you're at your worst, your most self-pitying, or your most depressed, the best thing you can do for yourself is to give back to others. Do something kind for someone else: Plan a party, give a gift, volunteer at a local organization, call a relative. Besides making yourself and someone else feel good, it's also an important reminder that the world does not begin and end with your pain. There's life out there, and it's up to you to engage with it.

ADOPT A [INSERT YOUR PET OF CHOICE HERE]

When Lindsey's boyfriend broke up with her, she immediately decided she needed a cat. "It was the best decision I ever made. I met with my therapist the following week and she was like, 'Um, you seem . . . good?' And I was like, 'Yes. I love my cat more than I ever loved my ex.'" She now has a giant painting of her cat above her living room couch, which features prominently on her dating app profile—which, naturally, results in tons of interest from exactly the kind of men she's into.

DO NOT, UNDER ANY CIRCUMSTANCES, TEXT THEM

Going "no contact" is quite trendy these days, if a little controversial. But when it comes to exes, it's kind of the only way. That means no texting, calling, meeting up, and no looking up their social media (once again, make ample use of that glorious mute button!). "The only way was to pretend he had never existed," says Caroline. "I didn't think about him, mention him, look at photos, anything."

Trust me, I get that this is a lot harder than it sounds. It is extremely difficult to go from texting someone all the time and knowing exactly where they are at every moment to suddenly treating them like a stranger. But that's what it takes when you're trying to move on. When you're in this stage, every time you have the urge to text them, text a trusted friend instead, or write in your Notes app what you would have sent. And leave it there.

The no-contact stage also might last a lot longer than you think. I'm one of those people who, despite assuring each other during every breakup that "We'll still be friends!," still hasn't figured out a way to maintain an actual friendship with an ex. That's not to say I'm on bad terms with any of them—if I saw them out in public, I like to think it'd be a cute, amiable encounter with only minor awkwardness—but we don't keep in touch. We've all moved on with our lives by now, and any closure I would have liked to have had at the time doesn't really matter anymore.

That's the thing you need to be able to ask yourself whenever you're overcome with the desire to reach out: What am I really after here? Am I just seeking the comfort of someone familiar? In that case, do something else that brings you familiar comfort. Watch your childhood favorite movie, call a best friend, make the meal your mom used to cook when you were sick.

Or are you reaching out because you're desperate to get the answers to the nagging questions keeping you up at night? In other words, are you seeking "closure"?

I'm gonna hold your hand when I tell you this (metaphorically), but "closure" doesn't actually exist. You will have many relationships in your life that veer in strange directions, that end abruptly, relationships where you get hurt or hurt someone else, relationships where one person changes and the other doesn't and it's never the same again. You will have a story about what happened, and so will the other person. Sometimes neither of you will be able to make sense of it at all.

But unlike in family or friendship scenarios, where there's far more gray area regarding the ways a relationship can evolve, in monogamous romantic breakups, only one thing matters: that one or both of you have chosen not to be together anymore. There can be a million little reasons or one big one. It's all the same. Because once you've broken up, there's only one path to go down, and it's the one where you're on your own. For better and for worse, they're not your problem anymore.

I know how tempting it is to try to show someone just how badly they hurt you. I know that during the hardest breakups, you'd give anything just to get the other person to understand how horrible you feel, and how it's all their fault. But just as they're not your problem anymore, you're not theirs anymore either. You're the only one who can help you now.

And finally, and most importantly, under absolutely no circumstances should you overthink it when they look at your Instagram

Story or like your posts. People will do this, even though it's weird. But trust me, it does not mean they want to get back together or that they're sending you signals in an effort to get you to reach out. Think of how many random people's posts you like or look at. How many of them are you secretly in love with? Exactly.

REMIND YOURSELF OF THE UNFORTUNATE, INEVITABLE TRUTH

If you wanted to, you could do everything on this list. I've tried and would recommend most of them. But there's only one method of getting over someone that actually works. And it's the most annoying fucking one of all.

It's time.

Think of your unrequited crushes from high school, all the times you never got asked to the dance, your most embarrassing failures from years past, the little rejections that seemed like world-ending catastrophes that you now look back on as either funny stories or pivotal moments of growth you're immensely grateful for. That's exactly how you'll look back on your worst breakup. You'll acknowledge that it was difficult, but you'll also be aware of how young you were—you are still so much younger than you think!—and that it turned you into the person you're supposed to be.

You're not going to feel this way forever, even if you think you will. The things that matter now won't matter in a year, two years, ten. However insane it sounds, you'll smile about this someday. And you'll be stronger for it, too. Someone might have dumped you from their island, but other people's islands are overrated anyway. You've got your own to build.

Key Takeaways:

- Heartbreak is the hardest part of dating, period. Give yourself time to grieve, even if other people don't get it. (Especially if what you're grieving was a situationship or a casual fling. These can be just as painful!)

- Travel, cut your hair, adopt a pet, throw yourself into a hobby, or the gym, or a project, or your community— distractions are your best friend.

- Do not, under any circumstances, text them. "Closure" doesn't actually exist. For better and for worse, they're not your problem anymore, and you're not theirs either.

- You can try every "get over him!" tactic in the entire world, but only one really works: time.

Seventeen

THE GOLDEN RULE

The most romantic thing anyone can do on *Love Island* is to leave the villa when their partner is dumped. You will not be surprised to learn that this is an extraordinarily rare occurrence; for the vast majority of islanders, the promise of more screen time (or the arrival of a new bombshell) is far more enticing than giving it all up for someone they've only known for a few weeks. But on the few occasions where this has happened, boy, does it make for good television—and if history is any indication, lasting relationships.

In season 2 of *Love Island* UK, Rachel and Rykard are voted by the public to be one of the two least compatible couples on the show, meaning that their fellow islanders will have to vote one of them out. After Rachel, the newer entry to the villa, is dumped, host Caroline Flack congratulates Rykard for making it through another day. But then he stops her.

"If you've got a good girl, mate, you can't really let her go," he announces. "So I'm out." He then turns and runs down the beach after Rachel and wraps his arm around her. "I can't just let you walk off. Fuck that shit. I'm here," he tells her. "What am I here for, to keep flirting?"

It's one of the sweetest moments I've ever seen on *Love Island*—impressive, considering the fact that Rykard had slept with another girl in the villa just days beforehand. "That's the nicest thing I've ever seen someone do," one of the other islanders remarks. "An absolute gent," says another.

It is also indicative of what I believe—with rare exceptions—to be the number one rule of dating: *If they wanted to, they would.*

This is somewhat controversial advice. There's something undeniably heteronormative and gender essentialist about it: In most cases, the phrase is used with male pronouns ("if he wanted to, he would"), therefore sneakily promoting the stereotype of the man-as-pursuer and the woman-as-object-to-be-pursued. Dating advice books from the '90s and 2000s are full of this kind of sentiment: that to understand men, you've got to understand their biological nature, that men are just predisposed to love the chase, that it's his hunter-gatherer instincts that push him to go after what he wants. What this implies to women is that it's our job to just sort of . . . sit there and wait around for someone to profess their undying love for us. And if it doesn't happen, welp, welcome to spinsterhood!

That's not the way I mean it. I don't believe all men love the "thrill of the chase" (in fact, I think many men would be psyched to get asked out), nor do all women envision their ideal dating scenario to be some kind of *Bridgerton*-esque courtship situation where your whole life involves sitting in your parlor room eating tea cakes and waiting for the doorbell to ring. (Well, maybe I'd still take the tea cakes. And the fashion.)

What I mean is that if you're dating someone and they like you, it should not be a mystery. You should not be overthinking everything you say, every awkward pause, every time it takes them a few hours to text back. Instead, your first thought should be a generous one: *Of course* they're taking a while to text back because they're busy doing something else. *Of course* that awkward pause wasn't a huge deal. You'll realize the small things actually are small things and not warning signs of a bigger future problem. You should know this because it should be obvious that they care about you despite all of the nonsense that human beings spiral over when they're in the first stages of dating.

Yes, these beginning phases can be super anxiety-inducing, especially if you're someone who overthinks every tiny interaction and is obsessively on the lookout for potential red flags. At the end of every date, you pore over everything that happened, whether you misread certain signals (or what the signals even were), whether you were a weird kisser, or whether they judged you for ordering a fourth drink.

Can you tell I'm one of those people? Because I absolutely am. When I first started dating my husband, I was looking for literally any sign that he wasn't that into me, and every time he showed me he did like me, I convinced myself that what he was giving me was straight out of the playbook taught in Fuckboy 101. I was deeply suspicious of him for an embarrassingly long amount of time, likely because I was dealing with the kind of self-esteem and trust issues that make me suspicious of anyone who purports to like me. The best way I can explain it is feeling like you're at a used car dealership and you get the sneaking sense you're being scammed. Like, what's the catch here? Am I just the only idiot in the world to fall for your organ-harvesting scheme?

This isn't a quality I'm proud of, but I do think it's the reason why, despite all my zillion flaws and the many mistakes I've made in my dating life, I've never seriously dated anyone who wasn't a little obsessed with me, even if the relationship didn't work out. Maybe it's because I've always hated competition (I would be a legendarily terrible *Love Island* contestant) and am famously a serial monogamist, but I simply could never be bothered to date someone who does not make their feelings about me very clear. To me, that's the bare minimum of a relationship: What's the point of being exclusive and spending all your time with someone who doesn't make you feel loved, cherished, and appreciated, and whom you don't feel the same toward?

That's the question I ask all of my friends when they've found themselves in new relationships: Are they obsessed with you? And are you obsessed with them? Often I don't even have to ask. You can just tell. You can see the way they look at each other, or the way one seems to orbit around the other even when they're across the room. But other times with friends who are more private or I don't see that often, that question is a way of helping them suss out whether this is someone they really want to be with, or whether they're simply settling for whatever's come along.

One clear signal that you've found the right person for you is that all of a sudden, and probably without even realizing it, you feel a strange sense of *calm*. The person doesn't have to "prove" their feelings toward you through any kind of grand gesture or public pronouncement, you can just feel it, without any of the pomp and circumstance.

And then there are the folks who absolutely despise this advice. "I can't stand it," says Virginia. "I think it's led women to create nearly impossible standards, and if someone doesn't behave exactly how they want, they cut it off. Ultimately no one is a mind reader and no one is going to know how you feel unless you say something."

She's not the only one. A 2022 *Glamour* magazine story deemed "if he wanted to, he would," which was going viral on TikTok at the time, "terrible advice," and that it ignores introverts, anxious people, or the socially awkward. Also, the story argues, it just feels mean. "What comes across is: That man doesn't want you. Get it through your head. If you keep trying to make something happen with him and he keeps treating you badly, that's on you. Now you're not only undesirable, you're also stupid."

I completely understand these criticisms. When you've been dating around for years, getting your hopes up for someone who turns out to suck, catching feelings only to get ghosted, or ending up in hazy situationships that leave you feeling small or used, the last thing you need to hear is that yet another person thinks you're worthless. It's hard enough being vulnerable with your friends when you're telling them stories about your dating life (especially if they're partnered up and therefore believe they're the world's number one expert on relationships). But when you're constantly hearing "if he wanted to, he would" from those you trust, it makes you feel rejected all over again. Plus, it places all of the power into the hands of the other person: Why should *you* feel bad over someone else's disinterest?

This is especially important when you understand that so many men don't know how to recognize something good when they get it. Men are *incredibly* adept at fumbling the best thing that ever happened to them. This is all to say that if a man doesn't put in as much effort as you'd like, or doesn't seem to be receptive to your needs, that does NOT mean you are undesirable or worthless. It just means that he hasn't yet learned to appreciate what's in front of him or communicate appropriately with people he's dating. There's a good chance you'll run into this kind of guy a lot in your dating life, which is why "if he wanted to, he would" is a useful way to suss them out.

The advice isn't supposed to make you feel like shit—it's supposed to remind you that even if society's standards for what counts as a "decent guy" are basically in the toilet, yours don't have to be. Someone who makes you feel anxious and uncomfortable and unsure of yourself all the time maybe isn't the right person for you, whether they're into you or not. And speaking of . . .

ON "HE'S JUST NOT THAT INTO YOU"

We have now reached the dreaded portion where I must bring up the dating advice everyone's probably sick of: "He's just not that into you." When the self-help book of the same name was published in 2004 (and again when the movie adaptation came out five years later), many critics panned the central thesis and the smarmy tone of its narrators. "This is dating for little girls," wrote one *Guardian* reviewer who referred to it as "pop cultural self-hatred," while *The New York Times* called it "obnoxious."

But in the twenty years since its publication, others have revisited the text and found a slightly more flattering portrait of what is ultimately pretty solid advice. A *Vice* review in 2020 concluded that *He's Just Not That Into You* holds up despite its fundamental heteronormativity and "bullshit evolutionary psychology," at the very least because it encourages self-respect: "A lot of us could stand to get better at recognizing and accepting a soft no from the people who are too uncomfortable or too shy or too lazy or too afraid or too over it to give a clear no." That way, the book argues, you're less likely to end up in relationships where you're constantly feeling rejected, hurt, and less-than.

I think this is advice that all genders can learn from (not least men, who famously have not been great at accepting rejection from women). The goal here is that you can avoid those kinds of fuzzy, confusing situationships in which you convince yourself that it's eventually going to lead to a fulfilling relationship but only ends up with you feeling like shit about yourself.

Trust me, I've been in plenty of those. And, I'll admit, I've been in situations where I knew the other person liked me a lot and wanted something more and I was the one who insisted on keeping things casual. I like to think that I was kind and respectful in those cases. But I'm sure I did some shitty things, too. I'd brush it off whenever they made any hint of romance, I'd sometimes ignore their texts, I'd only agree to hang out when it was most convenient for me or if I was feeling lonely.

Worse, I'd erected an invisible wall that kept them at arm's length at all times and deluded myself into thinking they couldn't feel it. But of course they could. Having been on the other side, I know how much it hurts to be on the receiving end of someone who clearly doesn't feel the same, someone who's only keeping you around because they want someone ready to go on the back burner. Maybe they're terrified of being alone, maybe they're particularly needy, hell, maybe they're just bored. I was probably all three.

But the point is that if I wanted to, I would have. I just didn't want to.

And the truth was, there was probably nothing the other person could have done to convince me otherwise. As is the case with most relationships, the more you try to force each other into a situation that doesn't come naturally, the more impossible it is to feel natural at all. I couldn't force the other person to like me less, just as they couldn't force me into liking them more.

That's not to say there's no gray area in dating. Obviously it would be great if everyone in the whole world went to therapy and healed themselves to perfection and was then able to ask for exactly what they needed and followed through on all their promises to each other. Sadly, this isn't the way the world (or even therapy) works, and it's not how human beings behave. You can't "cure" messiness or conflicted emotions.

Hence, the frustrating truth about dating: You can like someone and feel unsure whether you like them enough to pursue a relationship. That's actually super normal! The whole point is that in the beginning, you're still getting to know one another.

Because most people aren't totally obsessed with each other right from the start. I'd even argue that if someone is super obsessed with you right away, that's maybe a red flag that they're projecting a persona onto you that may or may not be based in any sort of reality. This is especially true if you're meeting someone on a dating app, where first encounters often feel like job interviews—a little stiff, a little awkward—and someone's coming on way too strong, or being too touchy or laudatory in a way that feels inauthentic. One of the flaws of "if he wanted to, he would" is that if you base all your relationships on that logic, you could end up with someone you're not into at all, or someone who's developed an entire personality for you without really getting to know the real you, or someone who's just straight-up giving stalker vibes.

This is where the inverse of "if he wanted to, he would" comes in handy: If *you* wanted to, would you? In other words, do you actually like the person you're dating, and if so, are you showing them? This can be tricky for a lot of women, in particular women dating men: Everything we've been told growing up is that a woman who makes her feelings known is desperate, delusional, needy, or a "stage five clinger," as another iconic reality show would describe it. That's because we're told that men assume all women are interested in them (or at least that they should be), and therefore it's a woman's job to play hard to get and activate their intrinsic "thrill of the chase" genes.

Again, this is an enormous generalization and a sweeping, misguided judgment about an impossibly large demographic. Yes, some men love the chase. But most of us, gender notwithstanding, just want to be with someone who likes us, someone we can feel free to be our full selves around and not worry they'll change their mind over a minor faux pas.

To that end, if you like someone, make it clear. Don't neglect the basics: Ask them questions, reply to texts in a timely manner, give them compliments. Buy a round of drinks; bring them coffee. Tell them little things that reminded you of them. Hold the door. Hold their hand. Make them a playlist. Take cute pictures of them. Plan a date with multiple stops (this is the most romantic thing anyone can ever do!). If you don't have the desire to do this stuff, chances are you don't really want to be in a relationship with that person. That's okay! But it is your job to be honest about that. And if you feel like you're that preheating pot waiting on the back burner that never seems to come to a boil, it's time to ask them what's up.

The best-case scenario, though, the kind every dater hopes for, is that within the first few weeks or months, you both realize you *want to*. You *want* to be talking to each other regularly, you *want* to be planning dates, you *want* to be introducing your friends and making out all over town. And mostly, you want to show the other person you care, because you've suddenly realized that playing it cool is way overrated.

Before Rykard and Rachel left the show, they had a sit-down conversation in which he explained why he followed her out the door. "When I saw you walk away, I just knew I had to get you," he said, before reading her a poem. Now that's a guy that *wanted to*.

We all deserve to be with someone who wants to be with us. If your person isn't making it clear, ask for what you want. And if they're still unsure of their answer, ask yourself this: If you got dumped from *Love Island*, would your person leave with you?

I can tell you right now that if they wanted to, they would.

Key Takeaways:

- I'll say it again: If they wanted to, they would.
- Men are, unfortunately for them, very adept at letting great people pass them by. If a guy you're seeing can't understand why you might need more than the bare minimum, that isn't a referendum on your worth. You are still desirable and hot and cool, even if some guy isn't making as much of an effort as you'd like.
- "He's just not that into you" can sometimes feel mean or regressive, but understanding what a subtle no looks like can be a really helpful way to avoid wasting your time on people who just aren't the one.
- You can't force anyone to like you more, just like nobody can force you to like them more (or less).
- When you like someone, make it clear. Women are often terrified of coming across as pushy or clingy, but many of us need a little encouragement from our partners in the early delicate stages of dating (even men)!

Eighteen

THE REAL WINNERS

We've spent this entire book talking about *Love Island*, a show where the purported goal has always been to couple up, maintain a strong relationship from the get-go, and earn the public's vote to win the £50,000 prize. It's right there in the name: *Love Island* is meant to be a show about finding love. In this, the franchise has been quite successful: Many couples who leave the villa remain together for years; some even get married and have kids (or three, in the case of Camilla and Jamie).

But that's not actually what *Love Island* is about. *Love Island* is a show where people enter the villa as one person and leave as a totally different one. The vast majority of the time, they walk in as unknowns—people who happen to look really hot in swimwear but hail from the middle of nowhere and have careers they're mostly ambivalent about. They're there for fun, for a shot at meeting their person, but most of all, they're there to change their life. They're there to emerge on the other side with hundreds of thousands of social media followers and a whole new world. Maybe they'll start a podcast, maybe they'll do sponsored content for a beauty brand or launch their own, maybe they'll be given the opportunity to guest on other reality TV shows—or become a host of *Love Island* itself.

And those islanders, the ones who leave the villa and build for themselves an entirely new life, who have taken this very bizarre, random opportunity and spun it into gold, are the real winners of *Love Island*. Not the ones who secure the £50,000 prize. And not the ones who get married at the end of it.

You would be forgiven for asking, "Isn't that kind of a depressing and materialistic way of looking at things?" And you would sort of be right. Life isn't—and shouldn't be—about getting a zillion Instagram followers. But it's also not just about focusing entirely on finding a partner at the expense of all the other things that make up a really wonderful, meaningful, well-rounded, romantic life. Your world does not need to revolve around the quest to find "your person."

I want to stress what an absolute privilege this is. Fifty years ago, an American woman couldn't open a credit card in her own name unless her husband cosigned. (If she didn't have a husband? Welp, too bad.) And it wasn't until the Affordable Care Act in 2010 that health insurance companies weren't allowed to discriminate against women by charging more. Workplaces were just as hostile: Until 1978, a woman could be fired for getting pregnant. Sexual harassment wasn't labeled as a form of discrimination until 1980. Most horrifying of all was the lack of control women had over their own bodies. Unmarried women couldn't legally get prescribed the birth control pill until 1972. And spousal rape wasn't criminalized in all fifty states until 1993—technically in my lifetime.

I'm not saying things are perfect now. In 2022, the Supreme Court overturned *Roe v. Wade*, the decision that legalized abortion in all fifty states. We're in the middle of an uphill battle to recoup some of that autonomy we thought would be protected for the rest of our lives. But things are significantly better than they once were, and it's worth being reminded that it is pretty damn cool to be a woman in an era where you're not basically required to have a partner. I know it's a cliché to be all like, "You're an independent woman who doesn't need a man!" But like, you *literally don't*. And that's a beautiful thing.

A world where women don't need men is a world where women don't settle for the first just-okay dude who comes along, one who promises financial and romantic security and bails as soon as things get tough. It's a world where women can build full lives that they love without men interfering in them or telling them they can't, a world where women get to put their personal achievements over traditional markers of adulthood like getting married or having kids. It's a world where women, in theory if not always in practice, get to plan a life where the only thing they have to worry about is their own joy, something so many women throughout history have never had the privilege to do.

The next time you're out on a Friday night with your friends, lamenting the dwindling options on the apps, commiserating about the disappointing dates you've been on lately, remind yourself of this: You are lucky enough to live in a time where being single doesn't make you a freak. Not that it ever did, obviously, but it's never been more of the case than right now. While it's true that our economic and civic structure is stuck in the past and most systems are still set up for couples, the act of being single is no longer some kind of major social transgression. More people are marrying later, if they choose to do so at all. You could lament this as some sort of cultural travesty, sure, but it also means that there are tons of people out there who are experiencing the exact same thing, who are rethinking what it means to live a good life. Singlehood isn't a *trap* you're confined to.

With that, I want to spell out all the other important things to remind yourself as you continue on your dating journey. Let this be a handy little list of mantras to come back to when things feel scary or confusing or chaotic or hopeless. Because it's never hopeless. You're meant to be right where you are, right here, right now.

NOT BEING FOR EVERYONE IS A GOOD THING.

Did you know it's *great* that some people won't like you? And that some of them might actually hate you? Even though I'm sure you've heard this a million times, it's shocking how difficult it is to really accept. When you're out there in the dating world, it can feel like every rejection is a sign that you're inherently unlovable, that no one will ever accept you for who you are or even take the time to get to know the real you.

It's a devastating feeling, but it's also a lie. Developing a strong sense of self and an identity outside romantic relationships means that you're not one of those people who simply mold themselves to whomever they're dating at the time. That's a huge sign of strength. Will it drive some people away or turn some of them off? Of course it will. But if it doesn't, you probably have a really boring personality, and that sucks for you! Embrace the part of yourself that's weird or quirky or "unlovable." It's the part that someday, someone might love the most.

NO ONE IS COMING TO SAVE YOU.

I mean this in the most liberating way possible: There is nobody who is coming to rescue you. Unlike pretty much everything we're told growing up, your life doesn't start when you meet your soulmate, and getting sucked into this kind of all-or-nothing mindset is a really good way of making yourself deeply unhappy.

"So many people think they will be 'complete' when they find a partner, and that is simply not true," says Virginia. "Find appreciation and gratitude for yourself and the love you already have."

A good way of reframing your perspective is to try to imagine a life where you don't end up having that romantic fairy tale of meeting "the one." What would that look like? How can you add joy, romance, excitement, and stability into your life, even if it doesn't end up looking like everybody else's?

Once you do that, it's much easier to follow what I think is the best approach to dating: by only considering people who are truly additive to your experience. If someone you're dating isn't making you happy or creating value for your life, leave them behind and return to the awesome, already-great world you've fostered for yourself. This is how pretty much everyone I know who's dating, especially in their thirties, operates, and it's kind of the only way to stay sane.

YOU DIDN'T "MISS THE BOAT."

You know those people who marry their high school sweethearts? Or met "the one" in college, or at their first job, or on Tinder? Those people, the ones we think of as lucky because they never had to endure the hellish process of dating, aren't as fortunate as you might be tempted to believe.

I'm not saying everyone who marries young will end up miserable, but in circumventing the dating world, they missed out on an element of modern life that can have really surprising and amazing effects. Dating—that is, meeting new people and seeing how they fit, over and over again—can help us become the version of ourselves we're meant to grow into. It can lead us across oceans, and introduce us to new hobbies, friends, cultures, and ways of existing. By not embracing serendipity, you're closing yourself off from so much that you might have never known was possible. No offense to anyone who never dated as an adult, because it has nothing to do with them as people, but I truly shiver thinking about what my life would look like if I ended up with one of the guys I dated in high school. And that's worth all the disappointment and rejection in the world.

YOU ARE ALLOWED TO TAKE AS MANY BREAKS AS YOU NEED.

Frustrated by dating apps? Starting to feel as though everyone in the world sucks and you'll never find love and also you're constantly feeling irritated and angry and no one, try as they might, seems to get it? Want to scream at the nearest coupled-up person who smugly tells you, "It'll happen when you least expect it!" These are all signs it might be time to take a break from dating. Don't worry. The streets will be there when you come back.

DISTRACTIONS ARE YOUR BEST FRIEND.

In the meantime, distract yourself into oblivion. Friends, creative projects, hobbies, home sprucing, a season of *Love Island* you've never seen before, deciding on a whim to try on a whole new personality, complete with a new fashion sensibility and musical taste— literally anything is a better use of your time than spiraling over people who aren't interested in you or succumbing to your anxiety about dating.

SAY NO WHEN YOU WANT TO SAY NO . . .

You are not obligated to go on a date with anyone you're not interested in. You are not obligated to *keep* dating anyone you're not interested in. You are not obligated to kiss, hook up with, or have sex with someone you're not really excited about doing those things with. Say no when it doesn't feel good, if you don't feel safe, or if you're simply not into it right now. You can say no to anyone, at literally any time.

. . . AND SOMETIMES EVEN IF YOU DON'T.

Trust me, I understand how tempting it can be to just say, "Fuck it!" and agree to meet up with someone who sends a "you up?" text past midnight after who-knows-how-many drinks. But "doing it for the plot" isn't always worth the twist that comes after. Before you agree to whatever risky behavior you're considering, try to imagine what advice a close friend might give you in this scenario. And try your best to listen.

SAY YES WHEN YOU WANT TO SAY YES . . .

Dating is fundamentally about openness. It's not about making a hundred-point list of attributes you'd like to have in your perfect partner and scouring the globe for a person who meets all of them. "Be open to meeting people who don't match up with your specifications," says Meredith. "If I only tried to date people that checked my boxes, I wouldn't have dated any of the people I've had meaningful relationships with."

Dating is a time when you should be saying yes to more things than not, and challenging yourself to get out of your comfort zone. "You simply have to put yourself out there," adds Charlotte. "You can't expect someone to just fall into your lap. This can look like a lot of different things—get yourself on the dating apps, go out to a bar with friends and try to flirt with people, join a class or get a hobby that would put you in contact with people you might want to date, or go up to that cute friend-of-a-friend at your friend's birthday party. You can't wait for the world to come to you." Make eye contact, smile at people, position your body so it's facing the crowd, have a go-to conversation starter (see chapter 2!), give compliments, and flirt with absolutely everyone.

. . . AND SOMETIMES EVEN IF YOU DON'T.

I know it feels like I've spent half the book harping on this, but I'm going to say it again: You really do need to be leaving your house. Even when you're so, so comfy and so, so tempted to spend another night under a big blanket watching reruns of your favorite show by yourself. Even when you know that the likelihood of you meeting "the one" when you say yes to a party or meetup with friends at a bar is close to zero. Because, yes, you're probably right, it's highly unlikely you'll meet your soulmate at any one moment in time. But it's good for you to be out there anyway.

THERAPY IS GOOD.

Loving yourself, even when it's really difficult, will help you so much in navigating the inevitable ups and downs of dating. And before you love yourself, you've got to know yourself. Seeing a therapist can be a crucial step in learning about what makes you tick, what you value, and the patterns you've been stuck in that might be holding you back from meeting and dating the right people.

Plus, ensuring you're in a solid, grounded place before diving head-first into dating will, as Tiana says, "help you not use a relationship as a Band-Aid for something." Therapy isn't the be-all, end-all of self-care, but it's a good place to start, especially when you're in that stage of feeling like you don't love yourself and worry that nobody ever will.

MOST PEOPLE AREN'T INHERENTLY EVIL.
WE'RE ALL JUST TRYING OUR BEST.

When you've been disappointed over and over again and get trapped in the same cycles, dating people who either end up rejecting you or who show themselves to be unworthy of a relationship, it's easy to feel like you've simply run out of options, and that all of them suck. It's like when you've run out of levels to beat in a video game, except way more depressing.

But it's a fallacy. The dating pool is always growing and changing as people exit relationships and put themselves back out there. And the vast, vast majority of them are just like you—wanting to find love, but also needing to stay true to themselves.

"I've realized with time and age that everyone is doing their best," says my friend Lydia. "Most men aren't narcissists, despite what social media says. People fuck up. It takes a lot of inner work to be able to operate this way, so it's not for the weak. I'm proud of my ability to continue to pick myself up and move on when things don't work out. It requires a lot of confidence and courage to date!"

She's right. It's much easier on our egos to gaslight ourselves into thinking that the person with whom we had a bad experience is secretly an evil sociopath. But when you believe everyone is out to ruin your life, you close yourself off to meeting new people and therefore being surprised by them and what they might bring into your life. In the end, you're only hurting yourself.

LOVE IS A RISK.

I cannot tell you how many times I told myself when I was single that once I was in a great relationship, everything else would fall into place. I'd never have any problems again, and life would be smooth sailing from there on out. Lmao.

This is, of course, hilariously wrong. (The same goes for "When I finally get my dream job/glow up/move cities, my life will be perfect" thinking.) You can achieve everything you've ever wanted, you can be the most karmically blessed person in the world, you can have money and love and friends and a gorgeous home, and at any point, all of it can be taken from you.

Amanda's therapist once told her, "You want love with an insurance policy. That doesn't exist! Risk is inherent to love." She realized that she was trying to make all the "correct" decisions in her dating life, constantly calculating the risk in each choice, thinking that if she did everything "right," she'd be rewarded with the "right" kind of relationship.

But that's not how life works. "I realized that in any relationship with another human being, and especially in romantic ones, you have to cede some level of control. You have to embrace that you might experience massive heartbreak, even if you do the 'right' thing! There's no avoiding risk in love. That's part of the terror, but it's also part of the beauty of opening yourself up to it again and again." I couldn't have said it better myself.

Finally, I'll leave you with this:

LIFE ISN'T LOVE ISLAND. IT'S BETTER.

Remember how I said the real winners of *Love Island* aren't the ones who end up with the prize money or a marriage? That the actual point of *Love Island* was to leave with a newfound sense of self, and that love is just a bonus? The same thing is true in normal life.

The real winners are the ones who know that they'll be okay no matter what, whether that means meeting the love of their lives and staying together forever or whether it means building a life full of friends, family, a fulfilling career, fun hobbies, exciting experiences, and a sense of self that transcends the material markers of what counts as "aspirational."

The real winners are the ones who remain open to finding love even when they've been fucked over and beaten down more times than they can count. The ones who don't give up on the idea that there really are good people out there, waiting for you to find them.

The real winners are the ones who can walk into any room, with or without a partner, and know they are the absolute shit. The ones who are charming, friendly, and confident, who believe they are deserving of unconditional love, even when it feels impossible.

Life isn't *Love Island*. There's no £50,000 prize at the end, no free ticket to a career as an influencer.

Because guess what? Real life is better than that. It's about building your very own island, one that exists exclusively for you to be the bombshell you are—coupled up, or not.

Time to crack on.

Key Takeaways:

- There's never been a better time to be single than right now. You are *so lucky* to be born in an era when women don't need to rely on men to have a wonderful, full, fulfilling life. Whenever you're spiraling over how difficult it is out there, remember it's kind of a miracle that we get to go on dates, hook up with people, go out with our friends, and celebrate life just for the hell of it. Nobody gets to tell us what to do.

- Lead with the mindset of yes—in other words, be open to life! Leave your house! Talk to strangers! Even if you're so, so comfy at home, and even if the person you're talking to doesn't meet every single one of the dozens of boxes you think you need to be checking off.

- The real winners of *Love Island* aren't the ones who end up with the cash prize, or the ones who find their life partners. They're the ones who used the show as a means of creating a whole new, wonderful life for themselves. And the winners of the real world are the ones who know that they're the absolute shit, whether they're coupled up or not.

Acknowledgments

This entire book was written in the span of two months while also working a full-time job in journalism. While I do not recommend anyone ever do this, there were so many people who made my sixty days of furiously slamming on my keyboard bearable, and at times genuinely fun.

First, thank you to Hana and Brittany at Simon & Schuster for thinking of me for this project and trusting me with your vision—and also for bridging the generational divide between the Gen Z dating world and my extremely washed thirty-two-year-old life. You two are so much fun to work with, and I couldn't have asked for a better editing duo for my first rodeo in publishing.

To Jen Marshall and Jen Gates at ACM, or as I call them in my head, The Jens, for being such incredible agents, advocates, and for patiently explaining everything about how the book world works. Every author needs a pair of Jens!

To my editors at *Vox*—Naureen, Julia, Meredith, and Swati—for allowing me to write a book about dating advice based on *Love Island* even though it isn't exactly "on brand." You've made me such a better writer, and I miss working with you all so much!

Most importantly, this book would not have existed if not for the twenty hilarious, smart, and lovely people who agreed to be quoted in these pages. I am so proud to call them my friends and am infinitely grateful they allowed me to borrow their beautiful brains for this book.

Thank you to Lindsey for being such a wonderful champion and resource for all my dating-related questions; to Laura for your stylish quips; to Megan and Haley for your hilarious (albeit opposing) takes on "golden retriever boyfriends;" to Kat for your incredible anecdote about the early stages of dating you-know-who; to Sasha for your creative flirting tips; to Tiana for your brutal honesty on "alpha" bros; to Caroline for your great advice on safety and break-ups, to Andrew for your openness and moral clarity; to Liza for your contagious wanderlust; to Clara, Sarah, and Desiree for your bang-on perspectives about love bombing and grand gestures; to Virginia for your frankness about the dismal state of dating; to Amanda for your thoughtful insight and vulnerability; and to Meredith for your relationship wisdom. A special thank-you to Sara, without whom chapter 13 would be but a sad husk of itself—thank you for trusting me with your story!

And thank you to the friends who understandably did not want their whole-ass government name in a book about dating. Thank you to "Sylvie" for your always entertaining stories about love in London and your infectious zeal for life, to "Zoe" for your adorable casino date story, to "Charlotte" for writing an absolute novel in my survey and therefore giving me so much great material to work with, and to "Lydia" for proving that sometimes soulmates can be platonic.

To Alex, who happened to be working on a book at the same time and became my coffee-shop buddy over many winter weekends, thank you for the quiet moral support! (And thank you to the many baristas and bartenders in Prospect Heights who provided a much-needed change of scenery to those long writing days.)

If we have ever gone on a date or made out on a dance floor, thank you for unknowingly providing me with the life lessons and wisdom (question mark) that populate this book. Cheers to . . . most of you.

To the entire cast of *Love Island* UK seasons 3 and 5: You were responsible for some of the most entertaining television I've ever seen in my life. I hope that wherever you are, you're rich and thriving.

To my parents, thank you for showing me what a wonderful relationship looks like and for always being so supportive of my career—even when it sometimes involves writing in great detail about my personal life. :)

And finally, a million thank-yous to Luke, who spent much of these two months taking care of me when I was too busy writing to cook or clean, while also dealing with my anxiety spirals about hitting my weekly word-count goals. I love you and I love our life more than words can describe. You make me feel like a bombshell every day.

Notes

INTRODUCTION (OR WELCOME TO THE VILLA)

xi. *Instead we spend more time*: Ian Ward, "He Diagnosed America's Trust Problem. Here's Why He's Hopeful Now," *Politico*, May 12, 2023, https://www.politico.com/news/magazine/2023/05/12/americans-trust-government-00096509.

xii. *"Trustworthiness lubricates social life"*: Robert D. Putnam, *Bowling Alone: The Collapse and Revival of American Community* (Simon & Schuster, 2000), 21.

xiv. *When I interviewed* Love Island *US's*: Rebecca Jennings, "How *Love Island* USA Became This Summer's Most Exquisite Trash," *Vox*, July 20, 2024, https://www.vox.com/culture/361755/love-island-usa-season-6-finale.

1: ARE THEY YOUR "TYPE ON PAPER," OR ARE THEY A SAD PHOTOCOPY?

4. *As Tara Suwinyattichaiporn, a professor*: Jordana Comiter, "Can Having a 'Type' Hold You—and Your Dating Life— Back?," *Women's Health*, May 18, 2024, https://www.womenshealthmag.com/relationships/a60803477/romantic-type-holding-you-back-dating.

6. *But he was also accused*: Bethany Minelle and Claire Gregory, "Women's Charity Issues *Love Island* Warning as Adam Collard Returns to Villa,"

Sky News, July 12, 2022, https://news.sky.com/story/love-island-womens -charity-issue-warning-to-itv-as-adam-collard-returns-to-villa-12650152.

3: BECOMING THE BOMBSHELL

26. *But as Liv Walker*: Lara Walsh, "The 'Love Island' Glam Room Was Actually Where the Magic Happened," *PopSugar*, August 19, 2024, https://www.pop sugar.com/beauty/love-island-glam-room-49387069.

4: "THE ICK" IS FOR BABIES

35. *One psychologist told* Time *magazine*: Angela Haupt, "The Psychology of Why We Get 'the Ick,'" *Time*, March 22, 2024, https://time.com/6958762 /why-you-get-the-ick-psychology.

42. *But as he once wrote*: Luke Winkie, "Zooey Deschanel and Ben Gibbard Were '500 Days of Summer' Come to Life," *InStyle*, October 1, 2022, https://www .instyle.com/celebrity/zooey-deschanel-ben-gibbard-breakup-timeline.

44. *Examples include imagining him*: Tom Haynes, "If You Want to Get Over a Boy, Imagine Him Doing These 35 Things and You Will," *The Tab*, July 16, 2020, https://archive.thetab.com/uk/2020/07/16/how-to-get-over-your-ex-166761.

45. *Speaking about her current husband*: Sarah O'Byrne, "Olivia Attwood: What Gave Her 'the Ick'?," *Heat World*, March 26, 2024, https://heat world.com/entertainment/love-island/the-ick.

5: ALL MOUTH

53. *The latter in particular can have*: Andrea Bonior, "7 Signs That a Partner's Jealousy Is a Problem," *Psychology Today*, March 8, 2022, https://www.psy chologytoday.com/us/blog/friendship-20/202203/7-signs-partners -jealousy-is-problem.

6: DOING THE MOST

62.   *As one psychologist explained to* The New York Times: Gina Cherelus, "What Is 'Love Bombing'?," *The New York Times*, January 10, 2022, https://www.nytimes.com/2022/01/10/style/love-bombing.html.

62.   *In other words, it's manipulative*: Kaitlyn Tiffany, "Am I Being Love Bombed? Are You?," *The Atlantic*, February 22, 2022, https://www.theatlantic.com/technology/archive/2022/02/love-bombing/622861.

7: YOUR PERSON WILL TREAT YOU LIKE A PERSON

68.   *Since Trump's election in 2016*: Lyman Stone and Brad Wilcox, "Now Political Polarization Comes for Marriage Prospects," *The Atlantic*, June 11, 2023, https://www.theatlantic.com/ideas/archive/2023/06/us-marriage-rate-different-political-views/674358.

69.   *Around the world in places like*: Jonathan Yerushalmy, "What's Behind the Global Political Divide Between Young Men and Women?," *The Guardian*, November 13, 2024, https://www.theguardian.com/us-news/2024/nov/14/us-election-donald-trump-voters-gender-race-data.

69.   *Some, like* The Washington Post: Editorial Board, "If Attitudes Don't Shift, a Political Dating Mismatch Will Threaten Marriage," *The Washington Post*, November 22, 2023, https://www.washingtonpost.com/opinions/2023/11/22/marriage-polarization-dating-trump.

8: TO SHAG, OR NOT TO SHAG

78.   *From Hannah and Jon's public bang sesh*: Hayley Minn, "Inside *Love Island*'s Steamiest Romps—from Pair Who Had Sex THIRTY Times to Star Who 'Went on Top for 20 Minutes,'" *The U.S. Sun*, January 9, 2023, https://www.the-sun.com/entertainment/tv-old/5483263/love-island-steamiest-romps-2022.

81.   *Sex therapists recommend talking out*: Elizabeth Enochs and Ali Drucker,

"11 Tips for Having Sex with Someone New," *Bustle*, May 28, 2021, https://www.bustle.com/wellness/tips-for-having-sex-with-someone-new.

82. *One study found that 58 percent*: Chanel Contos, "Sexual Choking Is Now So Common That Many Young People Don't Think It Even Requires Consent. That's a Problem," *The Guardian*, December 7, 2022, https://www.theguardian.com/commentisfree/2022/dec/08/sexual-choking-is-now-so-common-that-many-young-people-dont-think-it-even-requires-consent-thats-a-problem.

83. *"I've had friends who"*: "Condom Use Is Declining Among Younger Generations. Here's Why It's Become an Afterthought," *CBS News*, October 2, 2024, https://www.cbsnews.com/news/condom-use-declining-younger-generations.

9: I'VE GOT A TEXT (AND IT SAYS, "YOUR PHONE IS LYING TO YOU")

94. *Multiple studies have shown*: Tore Bonsaksen et al., "Associations Between Social Media Use and Loneliness in a Cross-National Population: Do Motives for Social Media Use Matter?," *Health Psychology and Behavioral Medicine* 11, no. 1 (2023), https://doi.org/10.1080/21642850.2022.2158089; Melissa G. Hunt et al., "No More FOMO: Limiting Social Media Decreases Loneliness and Depression," *Journal of Social and Clinical Psychology* 37, no. 10 (December 2018): 751–68, https://doi.org/10.1521/jscp.2018.37.10.751.

94. *Meta, Instagram's parent company*: Georgia Wells, Jeff Horwitz, and Deepa Seetharaman, "Facebook Knows Instagram Is Toxic to Teen Girls, Company Documents Show," *The Wall Street Journal*, September 14, 2021, https://www.wsj.com/articles/facebook-knows-instagram-is-toxic-for-teen-girls-company-documents-show-11631620739.

95. *As one psychologist explained to* Wired: Kenneth R. Rosen, "How to Stop Doomscrolling—with Psychology," *Wired*, March 30, 2022, https://www.wired.com/story/how-to-stop-doomscrolling-psychology-social-media-fomo.

95. *"Real-world relationships may help mitigate"*: Julia Ries, "How to Stop Con-
     stantly Comparing Yourself to Other People Online," *Self*, December 15,
     2022, https://www.self.com/story/social-media-comparison-tips.

98. *In an interview with* British Vogue: Sirin Kale, "'People Find Me Quite Con-
     troversial': Molly-Mae on Motherhood and Her 'Princess Diana and Charles'
     Level Break-Up," *British Vogue*, November 15, 2024, https://www.vogue
     .co.uk/article/molly-mae-british-vogue-interview.

10: MUGGED OFF BY THE ENTIRE WORLD

101. *"I still get trolling"*: Callum Wells, "'They Say I've Got a Big Tummy': Love Island's
      Liberty Poole Details Horrific Trolling Ordeal While Admitting She Broke
      Down in Tears After Being Heckled at Airport," *MailOnline*, November 6, 2022,
      https://www.dailymail.co.uk/tvshowbiz/article-11395693/They-say-Ive-got-big
      -tummy-Love-Islands-Liberty-Poole-details-horrific-trolling-ordeal.html.

102. *When she showed emotion*: Habiba Katsha, "*Love Island* Needs Black
      Women. Do Black Women Need *Love Island*?" *HuffPost* (UK), August 23,
      2021, https://www.huffingtonpost.co.uk/entry/love-island-needs-black
      -women_uk_611e3728e4b0c69681055fb2.

102. *It took four seasons to cast*: Katie Hind, "Is *Love Island* Racist? Viewers Turn
      on Dating Show After Male Contestants Ignore the Only Black Woman for the
      Second Year in a Row as Former Star Argues It Reveals the Shocking Truth
      About Modern Britain," *MailOnline*, June 8, 2019, https://www.dailymail
      .co.uk/tvshowbiz/article-7119851/Love-Island-viewers-turn-dating-male-con
      testants-ignore-black-woman.html.

102. *One season later, Yewande Biala*: Roisin O'Connor, "Yewande Biala Calls Out
      Fellow *Love Island* Contestant Lucie Donlan for 'Racialised Renaming,'" *The Inde-
      pendent*, January 23, 2021, https://www.the-independent.com/arts-entertainment
      /tv/news/yewande-lucie-donlan-love-island-feud-racism-b1791668.html.

102. *Meanwhile, fans pointed out*: Sarah Jones, "*Love Island* Viewers Complain
      That Yewande Is Getting Less Screen Time Than Co-Stars," *The Independent*,

June 10, 2019, https://www.the-independent.com/life-style/love-island-2019 -yewande-racism-contestants-missing-itv-a8949821.html.

102. *"We've seen nearly every Black woman"*: Katsha, *"Love Island* Needs Black Women. Do Black Women Need *Love Island*?"

102. *Data has shown that dating apps*: Liz Mineo, "How Dating Sites Automate Racism," *The Harvard Gazette*, April 4, 2024, https://news.harvard.edu /gazette/story/2024/04/how-dating-sites-automate-sexual-racism; Ashley Brown, "'Least Desirable'? How Racial Discrimination Plays Out in Online Dating," NPR, January 9, 2018, https://www.npr.org/2018/01/09/575352051 /least-desirable-how-racial-discrimination-plays-out-in-online-dating.

102. *One sociologist who interviewed dozens*: Kiara Byrd, "Black Women, AI, and the Dating App Dilemma," *Essence*, April 15, 2024, https://www.essence.com /lifestyle/dating-apps-black-women.

103. *Sarah Adeyinka-Skold, a professor*: Katelyn Silva, "Modern Dating as a Black Woman," *Omnia*, August 15, 2019, https://omnia.sas.upenn.edu /story/modern-dating-black-woman.

103. *In an essay for* Refinery29: Kelle Salle, "For Black Women, Dating Sucks. But That Doesn't Mean We Should Settle," *Refinery29*, April 5, 2024, https://www .refinery29.com/en-us/black-women-dating-settling-waiting-for-love.

104. *"Lots of people are willing"*: Aubrey Gordon, "When Your Fat Friend Dates," *Your Fat Friend*, March 12, 2016, https://www.yourfatfriend.com /home/2018/5/10/when-your-fat-friend-dates.

11: MAYBE THEY SHOULD CALL IT "FRIENDSHIP ISLAND"?

110. *Loneliness exacerbates the risk*: John Leland, "How Loneliness Is Damaging Our Health," *The New York Times*, April 20, 2022, https://www.nytimes .com/2022/04/20/nyregion/loneliness-epidemic.html.

111. *Thirty-six percent of Americans say*: "Loneliness in America: How the Pandemic

Has Deepened an Epidemic of Loneliness and What We Can Do About It,"
Making Caring Common Project, February 2021, https://mcc.gse.harvard.edu
/reports/loneliness-in-america; Daniel A. Cox, "The State of American
Friendship: Change, Challenges, and Loss," Survey Center on American Life,
June 8, 2021, https://www.americansurveycenter.org/research/the-state-of
-american-friendship-change-challenges-and-loss.

111. *On average, we spend less than three hours*: "Rebroadcast: Why Americans
Are Spending Less Time with Friends—and What to Do About It," *LAist*,
December 28, 2023, https://laist.com/news/npr-news/rebroadcast-why-americans
-are-spending-less-time-with-friends-and-what-to-do-about-it; Bryce Ward,
"Americans Are Choosing to Be Alone. Here's Why We Should Reverse That,"
The Washington Post, November 23, 2022, https://www.washingtonpost.com
/opinions/2022/11/23/americans-alone-thanksgiving-friends.

116. *In Lane Moore's book*: Lane Moore, "How to Find Your People," *Vox*,
April 25, 2023, https://www.vox.com/even-better/2023/4/25/23692759/how
-to-find-your-people-adult-friendship.

117. *After his time on the show*: Shivani Gonzalez, "When 'Love Island' Turns into
Friendship Island," *The New York Times*, August 16, 2024, https://www.nytimes
.com/2024/08/16/arts/television/love-island-rob-aaron-bromance.html.

12: PIED OFF

121. *One study of more than sixty couples*: Richard Sima, "These Science-Based
Tips Can Help You Manage Conflicts in Relationships," *The Washington
Post*, May 30, 2024, https://www.washingtonpost.com/wellness/2024/05/30
/relationships-conflict-management-settle-strategies.

121. *Other research shows that*: Amelia Hill, "Couples Who Argue Together, Stay
Together, Research Finds," *The Guardian*, February 13, 2018, https://www
.theguardian.com/lifeandstyle/2018/feb/13/couples-who-argue-together-stay
-together-research-finds.

13: TWO BIRDS, ONE VILLA

128.   *That's not to mention the several*: Gabriella Angelina, "10 of *Love Island*'s
       Most Notable LGBTQ+ Islanders," *Out*, July 24, 2024, https://www.out
       .com/gay-tv-shows/love-island-lgbtq-contestants-islanders.

131.   *Because in actuality, there are*: Emily Tomasik, "For Pride Month, 6 Facts
       About Bisexual Americans," Pew Research Center, June 28, 2024, https:
       //www.pewresearch.org/short-reads/2024/06/28/for-pride-month-6-facts
       -about-bisexual-americans.

132.   *Katie Salmon from* Love Island *season 2*: "*Love Island* Star Katie Salmon Says
       She Received Backlash from LGBTQ+ Community over Sophie Gradon
       Relationship," *Digital Spy*, September 25, 2018, https://www.digitalspy.com
       /tv/reality-tv/a866984/love-island-katie-salmon-backlash-lgbtq-communi
       ty-sophie-gradon-relationship.

14: BEWARE OF DOGS (AND OTHER TYPES OF MEN)

140.   *"Fine, I Admit It"*: Kayla Kibbe, "Fine, I Admit It—I, Too, Would Like a
       Golden Retriever Boyfriend," *Cosmopolitan*, December 5, 2023, https:
       //www.cosmopolitan.com/sex-love/a46030906/golden-retriever-boyfriend.

140.   Elle *put together a list*: Ruman Baig, "10 On-Screen Golden Retriever Boy-
       friends That Make Us Repulse the Bad Boys," *Elle India*, December 8, 2022,
       https://elle.in/10-on-screen-golden-retriever-boyfriends-to-crush-on.

17: THE GOLDEN RULE

168.   *A 2022* Glamour *magazine story*: Jenny Singer, "'If He Wanted To, He
       Would' Is Horrible Relationship Advice," *Glamour*, June 23, 2022, https:
       //www.glamour.com/story/if-he-wanted-to-he-would-dating-advice.

170.   *"This is dating for little girls"*: Tanya Gold, "We're Just Not That Into You," *The
       Guardian*, February 10, 2009, https://www.theguardian.com/commentis
       free/2009/feb/10/hes-just-not-that-into-you; Manohla Dargis, "Film Review:

He's Just Not That Into You," *The New York Times*, February 13, 2009, https://www.nytimes.com/2009/02/13/arts/13iht-flik14.1.20177238.html.

170. *A Vice review in 2020*: Rachel Miller, "Love/Hate Reads: 'He's Just Not That Into You,' Revisited," *Vice*, February 13, 2020, https://www.vice.com/en/article/hes-just-not-that-into-you-book-revisited.

18: THE REAL WINNERS

176. *Fifty years ago, an American woman*: Jessica Hill, "Fact Check: Post Detailing 9 Things Women Couldn't Do Before 1971 Is Mostly Right," *USA Today*, October 28, 2020, https://www.usatoday.com/story/news/factcheck/2020/10/28/fact-check-9-things-women-couldnt-do-1971-mostly-right/3677101001.

About the Author

REBECCA JENNINGS is a features writer at *New York* magazine. Previously she worked at *Vox*, where she covered social platforms and the creator economy with a focus on how social media is changing the nature of fame, fashion, money, and human relationships. Her work has explored everything from the joy of reality television to the rise of TikTok and why it feels like suddenly everyone's an influencer now. She lives in Brooklyn with her husband and cat.